How to Educate a Citizen

How to Educate a Citizen

The Power of Shared Knowledge to Unify a Nation

❖

E. D. Hirsch, Jr.

HARPER

An Imprint of HarperCollinsPublishers

HarperCollins books may be purchased for educational, business, or sales pro-
motional use. For information, please email the Special Markets Department at
SPsales@harpercollins.com.

FIRST EDITION

Designed by Kyle O'Brien
Charts by Nick Springer/Springer Cartographics LLC

Library of Congress Cataloging-in-Publication Data has been applied for.

ISBN 978-0-06-300192-3

20 21 22 23 24 LSC 10 9 8 7 6 5 4 3 2 1

The Education of youth is, in all governments, an object of the first consequence. The impressions received in early life, usually form the characters of individuals; a union of which forms the general character of a nation.

—Noah Webster, "On the Education of Youth in America" (1788)

The human being is less endowed with instincts for his guidance than the lower orders of animated creation.

—Horace Mann, *The Common School Journal* 1, no. 1 (November 1838)

The Swiss may speak four languages and still act as one people, for each of them has enough learned habits, references, symbols, memories, patterns of landholding and social stratification, events in history, and personal associations, all of which together permit him to communicate more effectively with other Swiss than with the speakers of his own language who belong to other peoples.

—Karl W. Deutsch, *Nationalism and Social Communication* (1953)

Contents

PART I
The Decline of the Common School

CHAPTER 1

When Our Schools Abandoned Commonality, We Became a Nation at Risk

I write this farewell book about American early schooling not just as an educator concerned about the quality of our children's education, but as an American concerned about our survival as a high-achieving, fair, and literate society. Over my long life, I have always been a booster of the United States, ever grateful for the blessings of liberty secured to us by our Constitution. No nation is without failure or shame, but I believe ours to be the best nation on earth—and not just for its spacious skies and amber waves of grain, although these do add to the sense of greatness and possibility. Along with our Constitution, it has been the schoolmistresses and schoolmasters of our past—starting with Noah Webster—who have kept us thriving and unified.

The nation-sustaining enterprise of our schoolteachers must be revived. If this book succeeds in conveying the old message in a new way—a message now validated by recent science—it will joyfully belong to that genre of book that succeeds in elevating rationality and natural science above emotional and religious sentiments of self-righteous certitude and moral indignation. The most recent, quite remarkable science reported in this book should help in that aim. Current brain research and current studies of language show that ethnicity and nationality are far from innate and exclusive properties. Ethnicity and nationality are written on our young neocortical blank slates by adults and experience.

Many Americans have gained more than one ethnicity. Those blank slates, as it turns out, can accommodate multiple ethnicities and identities. The currently popular term "identity," regarded as being immutable by birth and experience, is an inadequate concept. The essence of nationality and ethnicity inheres in a speech community that is based on shared knowledge. We must hope that recent scientific determinations (such as the discovery that the brain area where identity and ethnicity reside begins as a blank slate that our parents, our schools, and our surrounding culture write on) will induce a calmer, more productive consideration of what effective nation making and nation sustaining must entail. That is especially pertinent to our multiethnic nation that was once a symbol of human hope, and can be again.

For decades, I've been a rather polite scholar devoted to explaining how America's public schools, particularly at the elementary level (which is the focus of this book), are failing to educate our children effectively. The elementary school is decisive for forming both our knowledge base and our gut allegiance. Since the 1960s, our schools have been relying on a "progressive" approach called "child-centered learning" promoted and promulgated by our graduate schools of education. Education officials indoctrinated by those ideas set school standards that are unspecific with regard to content. Teachers, similarly indoctrinated, have gradually abandoned teaching knowledge coherently in favor of teaching mush on the scientifically incorrect premise that they are imparting general reading skills and general critical-thinking skills. But by neglecting their citizen-making duties, they are in fact diminishing our national unity and our basic competence.

History, geography, science, civics, and other essential knowledge that is the mark of an educated citizen have been dumbed down by vacuous learning "techniques" and "values-based" curricula. The results have been devastating: It's not simply a matter of ignorance (71 percent of Americans believe that Alexander Hamilton was president of the United States). The result is also the loss of a shared knowledge base across the nation that would otherwise enable us to work together, understand one another, and make coherent, informed decisions at the local and national level.

The costs of a broken approach to schooling leave our children underprepared and erode the American Dream. But there's an even deeper cost. Without schooling that teaches shared knowledge, the spiritual bonds that hold our society together are loosened. Arthur M. Schlesinger Jr. put it this way in *The Disuniting of America*: "The bonds of national cohesion are sufficiently fragile already. Public education should aim to strengthen those bonds, not to weaken them. If separatist tendencies go on unchecked, the result can only be the fragmentation, re-segregation, and tribalization of American life." Public discourse becomes increasingly uninformed and vitriolic, belief in political leadership dramatically declines, and disagreement over policy is translated into demonization of the other.

In the nation as a whole there is now a knowledge gap, a communications gap, and an allegiance gap. We don't understand one another; we don't trust one another; we don't like one another. Every Fourth of July, the Gallup poll reports a further decline in American patriotism and national pride. It has become fashionable to question patriotism and contrast it with a nobler globalism. But I believe Émile Durkheim was right to say that the nation-state is the largest possible unified social entity. Recent history has backed him up. We need global cooperation—yes, but Teddy Roosevelt was deeply right to say that the best contributors to international well-being and cooperation are unified, patriotic nations.

Failed Schooling and an Angry Population

Without the anchor of commonality in schooling that we largely had up to the 1940s, our ship of state is heading for a crash that it may not survive. There is already talk of secession. In 2017, in California one-third of polled voters said they would support their state declaring independence and becoming a separate country. In 2016, over a quarter of Texans said the same thing. Other states have prosecession groups campaigning to break away from the union. And while these impulses are not specifically tied to education, only an educated and patriotic citizenry can reverse this impulse.

This book will show that our loss of cohesion is partly owing to a loss of commonality in what we teach and therefore in what we know. At both the local and national level, an economy and a democracy can work effectively only if people understand one another. Language specialists use the term "speech community" to describe a group of people who share a set of language norms that allow them to interact, share interests, and participate in a healthy community. On a national level, this commonality is missing. The American Dream—the belief, unique to our nation, that anyone can rise from humble origins to achieve success—is fast becoming an American fantasy.

I addressed this politely in my initial critique, *Cultural Literacy* (1987), but it was met with the kind of fierce uproar from education professors and columnists that one would expect to be launched against a dangerous subversion of American liberties and social progress. Since the book was in its substance a report on the latest news from cognitive psychology, I was surprised at the ideological protest.

What it came down to was this: That earlier book contained a list of five thousand subjects and concepts that I suggested every child should learn. My critics denounced the list as elitist because of the number of "dead white males" featured as subjects. There was a prevailing movement—which I applaud in theory—to make the educational canon more multicultural. Anyone who suggested teaching the old canon was written off as reactionary.

The problem with this movement was that, while it was well meaning (and in the long run doable if done systematically and openly), the helter-skelter approach of its implementation has been particularly unhelpful to disadvantaged students. Because an intergenerational national culture grows and changes gradually, even in the internet era, the new schemes were not providing children with the knowledge they needed to learn to function effectively in society. And as this book will show, our elementary schools have not provided an even playing field for disadvantaged children.

Advantaged children gain much of that necessary knowledge outside school. But *all* children in a democracy devoted to equal opportunity and self-government need to understand key concepts, historical figures, and events if they want to succeed as functional and prosperous citizens.

Any attempt to change the shared canon by sudden fiat can work only if done methodically under broad agreement. You cannot swoop in locally, hack away at a nation's taken-for-granted understandings, and replace them overnight in your local school. It can't work, and it hasn't worked. When one school adds certain lessons for the sake of diversifying its curriculum and other schools add different lessons of their own, we're left with divided citizens who cannot communicate with one another, because they don't have enough knowledge in common.

Critics assumed that I was a conservative elitist trying to leave minority and disadvantaged students out of the conversation. The reverse was true: the aim is to give *all* students an equal opportunity to succeed by ensuring they have a curriculum that matches the cultural reality of the print culture (and now internet culture) in the public sphere.

But despite the hostility of the late 1980s, I continued to compose books and articles and gathered more scholarly and empirical evidence showing that shared knowledge is the right way to go. As I enter my tenth decade of life, and as I survey the increasingly disunified landscape that constitutes America's current culture and politics, I realize that my focus may have been too narrowly centered on pedagogy. In this book I take a broader view. I'm also more forthright and impatient, because things are getting worse. Intellectual error has become a threat to the well-being of the nation. A truly massive tragedy is building.

The National Need for Commonality

Schooling in a democracy is not just schooling. It's also citizen making. The United States' chief and earliest schoolmaster, Noah Webster (1758–1843), put it this way: "The Education of youth is, in all governments, an object of the first consequence. The impressions received in early life, usually form the characters of individuals; a union of which forms the general character of a nation."

National cohesion had been Noah Webster's great aim in the 1780s. He foresaw that the modern style of American democracy would have to be a manufactured thing, founded on a common system of laws, values, ethics, and a shared print language—what we call "culture" and that he called "manners." He foresaw that the new nation could work effectively only if its language and ideals and loyalties were commonly shared throughout the land.

He considered his effort to unify and level the United States culturally as a necessary element in creating a "people." His tradition, which led to a lot of commonality in our elementary schools, was key to our past unity and our high reading scores. Webster rightly understood that a common language and its

shared values learned in school were just as important to the
success of the new nation as its Constitution and formal laws.
He put it this way:

> A fundamental mistake of the Americans has been that
> they considered the revolution as completed when it was
> but just begun. Having raised the pillars of the building,
> they ceased to exert themselves and seemed to forget that
> the whole superstructure was then to be erected. This
> country is independent in government but totally depen-
> dent in manners.

"Manners" was civics and ethics and traditions and language
wrapped together. "Manners" was the normal word used in
the eighteenth century to translate the Latin word *mores*, as
in Cicero's famous "*O tempora O mores*" ("O the times, O the
manners"). The word "manners" embraced the whole range
of customs, values, and ethical rules, plus patriotic sentiments.
(Cicero in ancient Rome was complaining about the decline of
patriotism.)

Webster's hunch about the connection between language
and "manners" became a chief theme of twentieth-century
psycholinguistics. His ideas were also precursors of modern so-
ciolinguistics, which have determined that silently shared, unspoken knowledge and values are necessary to make a language
work. Webster understood that not just the language but also
the "sentiments" of the people had to be unified. He conceived
that our supertribe could work only if its members agreed to
its universal founding principles, obeyed its laws, and spoke the
same language. So pioneering and cogent was Webster's work

that most later nations adopted his ideas. Those nations are now typically monolingual republics based on written constitutions and school-promulgated standardized print languages.

But Webster, like Horace Mann, the founder of the common school movement in the 1830s, experienced opposition. Consistently in our history, the push for commonality in the United States has been resisted by two factions: first, by those who feel left out of the dominant culture; and second, by those who are opposed in principle to dull, unproductive uniformity. In the early nineteenth century, some of the opponents of the movement were Catholic leaders who feared that the common school was dominantly Protestant. Those who had more secular objections were those who considered uniformity the enemy of innovation and vigor.

But to *that* kind of pragmatic objection there is an even stronger pragmatic answer: commonality in the means of communication and in the valuation of liberty is consistent with high diversity in the *use* to which such commonality is put. Alexander Hamilton was right to make the dollar the common national currency. Similarly, Webster was dead right that we also need a common intellectual currency.

Not until after Webster's death did scholars recognize fully what he had accomplished for the nation—even beyond his *American Dictionary of the English Language*—through his schoolbooks, especially his so-called *Speller*, a small guide to American spelling filled with moral tales and sentiments and factual information about the new nation. This and his other schoolbooks, along with those of Caleb Bingham, were the means through which the language of the nation and its social values and commitments could be taught to all and shared by all.

On the publication of Webster's revised dictionary in 1828, James Kent, one of his admiring contemporaries and a distinguished contributor to the *Federalist* papers, stated that Webster was one of the three prime makers of America, to be ranked alongside Christopher Columbus and George Washington. That hyperbole was in a way deeply right—but with this proviso: He contributed more than just a dictionary. He helped found the American democracy.

As his new spellings and definitions took hold, so did the moral instructions and fables in his schoolbooks. These were usually devoid of literary merit, but Webster made it clear to the teachers and students who used the *Speller* that the unity of language in the nation ought to accompany high effort, honesty, and care for one's fellow citizens of all ranks and conditions.

> Be kind to all as far as you can; you know not how soon you may want their help; and be aware he that has the good will of all that know him shall not want a friend in time of need.

Such civic maxims were combined with stories whose moral and civic import was never in doubt: "The Boy that went to the Wood to look for Birds' Nests When he should have gone to School."

Webster's *Speller* was probably the most important schoolbook in US history, to be rivaled only by the McGuffey graded readers. In the early nineteenth century, Webster's blue-backed *Speller* found its way into almost every American classroom. By

1880, thirty-seven years after Webster's death, William H. Appleton, whose firm also printed Webster's dictionary, wrote that the *Speller* continued to command "the largest sale of any book in the world except the Bible." It sold more than a million copies a year—in large cases delivered to distributors who placed them "in every cross-roads store in the country."

A biographer of Webster, Harlow Unger, states that by 1900, after being a bestseller for more than a century, the Speller had sold over one hundred million copies, with an accurate count made impossible by the great number of unauthorized pirated editions. The thin, blue-backed speller was not enough, of course. Many other elementary-school readers—culture makers all—followed. These successors, along with Webster and newspapers, were important cocreators of the American public sphere, our shared knowledge and values.

So, it was Webster's schoolbooks *plus* his dictionary that bound the new nation together. With his schoolbooks he deliberately set about to create an American culture of equality, a prerequisite for political and social equality. Webster explicitly advocated a universal education for "all ranks of society."

And he succeeded. By the early nineteenth century, only one nation of the world, the United States, had a fully standardized, universally intelligible oral and print language. Ten years after Webster's death, a newspaper editorialist wrote the following in praise of his accomplishment:

The Yorkshireman cannot talk with a man from Cornwall. The peasant of the Ligurian [Italian] Apennines drives his goats home at evening over hills that look down over six provinces none of whose dialects he can speak. Here in America, five thousand miles change not the sound of a word. Around every fireside, and from every tribune, and in every field of labor, and every factory of toil, is heard the same tongue. We owe it to Webster.

Horace Mann and the Common School

The idea of a free, all-inclusive school system was originally conceived by Thomas Jefferson, a southerner who proposed a bill in Virginia that would have established schools every five to six square miles. In the fragile new American republic, education would no longer be available only to the rich. But Jefferson had little success with his efforts, which were thought in 1778 to be too radical. Then in the early nineteenth century, what became known as the common school movement, led by Horace Mann and other notables, took hold in the northeastern states and the Midwest. The common school was intended as the chief instrument of national cohesion and unity for "all ranks of society." The northerners who developed the common school in Massachusetts and Rhode Island were egalitarians who were deeply opposed to slavery.

Horace Mann's ideas spread far beyond Massachusetts, where he was head of the school board and editor of the nationwide *Common School Journal*, the most influential educational journal in US history. The schooling aims set forth in that publication were inspiring. Its multiple contributors agreed that educating "all ranks of society" to be readers, writers, and speakers with a shared allegiance to equality and fairness would be the necessary foundation of a prosperous, stable nation.

The common school movement did not directly specify a sequence of grade-by-grade topics, but nonetheless that is the way it usually turned out, because Webster's blue-backed *Speller* was gradually overtaken in the nineteenth century by the so-called readers of William McGuffey. These were "graded readers," meant to be taught in the grade levels specified in their titles. They expanded the work Webster had begun. They were earnest, high-minded, well-written books, which by the time a student encountered them in grade five became highly demanding conceptually and linguistically. The McGuffey readers were true citizen makers.

A New Birth of Freedom

According to the nineteenth-century advocates of the common school, the commonalty and universality of schooling were the only true guarantors of national unity, the only proper foundation for an admirable society. Yet since the northern idea logically implied the education of blacks, the South continued to resist. Economic dependence on slavery made the idea of educated blacks seem dangerous to southerners' way of life, as it undoubtedly was. By the time of the Civil War, the general educational level of the average person in the North was much higher than that in the South, judging by the lower percentages of school attendance in the southern states.

Before and during the Civil War (1861–1865), the South, morally infected by slavery, argued for the virtues of *non*commonality. According to Southern ideology, a free Confederacy was in principle more democratic than a "despotic" Union. Lincoln in his great speech at Gettysburg took the view that the

South's treasonous disobedience of the national Constitution put democracy itself at risk. The war was to determine whether this nation or any nation conceived in liberty and dedicated to the equality of all its people could long endure. Was real democracy—government by the people—a viable idea? The best thinking in the North was: "Yes, indeed it can be, if the American idea of embracing all people of all colors and ethnicities is accompanied by a common devotion to the national well-being—patriotism—and a common language."

In the mid-nineteenth century in the North, American national unity was understood and celebrated as containing multitudes, with unity sustained by the common school. American diversity was celebrated by Walt Whitman, for example, in his catalogs of American occupations, races, and nationalities. Whitman was in his youth a schoolteacher of multiethnic New York children. Herman Melville's great *Moby-Dick* symbolized multiethnic America in a whaling ship, the *Pequod*, a Native American name. The ship brought together all the ethnicities of the world—echoing Whitman's vision of unity in multiplicity—as did the American flag itself. The idea was that you could be an assimilated American without forgoing your ancestry or individuality. But there was this proviso: You had to go to school. Your children had to go to school. They had to learn to read, write, and speak the language, and gain a loyalty to the United States. They had to master McGuffey.

To see the common school as an agent of unity was a vision that teachers and writers of schoolbooks continued to hold through the first half of the twentieth century. Here is a statement of the social goals that guided Franklin Baker and Edwin

Thorndike, the editors of a widely used school anthology in the early to mid-1900s:

> We have chosen what is common, established, almost proverbial; what has become indisputably classic, what in brief every child in the land ought to know, because it is good and because other people know it. And it is well to remember what is old to us is new to the child. . . . In an age when the need of socializing and unifying our people is keenly felt, the values of a common stock of knowledge, a common set of ideals is obvious. A people is best unified by being taught in childhood the best things in its intellectual and moral heritage. . . . An introduction to the best of this is one of our ways of making good citizens. Not what we *know* only, but what we have *felt* and *enjoyed*, helps to determine what we are.

Educators in the 1920s, 1930s, and 1940s were still civic centered. They understood that commonality of knowledge and sentiment was essential to national effectiveness and comity. The ideal of the common school still dominated American early education. It had worked, and continued to work, and in the first half of the twentieth century, our young students and adults were rated at the top or near it in their ability to read and communicate.

But that was not to last. By 1950, with the retirement of older teachers and textbooks, a new educational theory, focused on the child rather than the nation, had taken hold. The common school had given way to the child-centered school.

The Child-Centered School and
American Romanticism

It is impossible to grasp the reasons for our national educational decline without understanding how our entire system of elementary education became hypnotized over several decades by a theory that viewed good education as being a "natural" development that should be conducted in accord with an individual child's nature and interests. I call this theory "educational romanticism" because it had its origins in the intellectual currents that were overlapping American thinking during the period following the Revolutionary War. By scholarly agreement, the new orientation is called "Romanticism."

It's the intellectual successor to the Enlightenment. The Enlightenment, with its faith in logic and science to advance the human condition, had created the United States. Jefferson and Franklin had been its children. The Enlightenment had also produced the common school, under the logical view that a common system of language, laws, and ideals would enable the new person—the American—to weaken or break the old ethnic bonds and form a thriving new nation.

At the turn of the nineteenth century, in the wake of the enthusiasm engendered by the American and French Revolutions, philosophers and poets began to see human progress as part of a natural, divinely ordained forward march of historical events. That's the essence of the German Romantic philosophers Friedrich Schelling and Georg F. W. Hegel—a natural, God-infused process onward and upward. Nature, including the unspoiled nature of the child, was seen as God's agent in this march of progress.

Human history was conceived to be progressive, to advance

naturally on its own, guided providentially by the inner necessity of Nature. That was the origin of the term "progressive education." For, with nature as our guide, the educational progress of the human child was to go forward naturally in the same positive manner—so long as we deferred to a providential Nature. "Nature knows best." The essence of educational romanticism is the idea that education should be individualized to accord with the child's nature. This meant that teachers were to vary school subjects to match up with the inherent natural interests of the individual child.

Elizabeth Peabody, the founder of the American kindergarten, once traveled to Germany in the nineteenth century to absorb the latest ideas of the German Romantic philosophers. She had already borrowed the German word *Kindergarten* for her early-age school. *Kindergarten* literally means "children garden." The aim of the "children garden" is to nurture the child's natural "growth," just as we nurture plants in a botanic garden—not by imposing formal external designs, but by encouraging the plant's natural development. This came to mean, especially in the crucial subject of language arts, the teaching of different content to different children—precisely the opposite of what is needed to engender shared knowledge.

But it took a long time for Romantic individualism to take over the common school. First, the older teachers and administrators had to die off. It was not until the early twentieth century that the new naturalistic, individualistic point of view, led by the philosopher John Dewey, began fully to take hold. And it was not until the early and mid-twentieth century that "progressivism" became dominant in US teacher-training institutions. Under the new conception, language instruction was no longer to be based on common subject matter, but rather on topics addressed to each child's strengths, weaknesses, and interests. The most "authentic" learning, we were told, must come from the child's "instincts and powers," as Dewey phrased it. The child was to choose what story to read, and to "construct" her own learnings, pursue her own "projects."

The romantics fell into a quasideification of the young child as being close to nature and therefore a kind of instinctive demigod. William Wordsworth (John Dewey's favorite poet) explains why the Romantics saw the child as a kind of oracle:

> Our birth is but a sleep and a forgetting;
> The Soul that rises with us, our life's Star,
> Hath had elsewhere its setting
> And cometh from afar;
> Not in entire forgetfulness,
> And not in utter nakedness,
> But trailing clouds of glory do we come
> From God, who is our home:
> Heaven lies about us in our infancy!
> Shades of the prison-house begin to close
> Upon the growing Boy,
> But he beholds the light, and whence it flows,
> He sees it in his joy;
> The Youth, who daily farther from the east
> Must travel, still is Nature's priest,
> And by the vision splendid
> Is on his way attended;
> At length the Man perceives it die away,
> And fade into the light of common day.

And more succinctly:

> *The Child is Father of the Man,*
> *And I could wish my days to be*
> *Bound each to each in natural piety.*

Being close to God, the young child possesses instincts that will be attracted to the stories and subject matters that are right for him. This theory—or theology—turned out to be incorrect.

By the 1960s its effects began to show up in the declining verbal scores of our middle school and high school graduates. For language mastery depends not on diversity but on commonality of knowledge. Under the new philosophy, we began to see a reduction of knowledge generally, and of shared knowledge in particular. Later, we began to see a decline in reading and social communication across the nation. "Progressive education," with its stress on "project-based learning," began falling into disrepute, because children were not learning very much. We began using the new phrase "child-centered learning." The name changed, but the chief view remained the same: Nature—the child's nature—knows best.

But common sense says (and I hope the reader agrees): grown-ups know best.

The Drop in Reading Scores

A bomb dropped in 1983 under the presidency of Ronald Reagan, with the release of a government report about the decline of our verbal scores. It was entitled *A Nation at Risk: The Imperative for Educational Reform*, and was terrifying in its alarm.

We report to the American people that while we can take justifiable pride in what our schools and colleges have historically accomplished and contributed to the United States and the well-being of its people, the educational foundations of our society are presently being eroded by a rising tide of mediocrity that threatens our very future as a Nation and a people. What was unimaginable a generation ago has begun to occur—others are matching and surpassing our educational attainments.

If an unfriendly foreign power had attempted to impose on America the mediocre educational performance that exists today, we might well have viewed it as an act of war. As it stands, we have allowed this to happen to ourselves. We have even squandered the gains in student achievement made in the wake of the Sputnik challenge. Moreover, we have dismantled essential support systems which helped make those gains possible. We have, in effect, been committing an act of unthinking, unilateral educational disarmament.

An act of war? The authors confirmed that they meant it to be as terrifying as it sounds. They meant it to get our attention—and it worked to good effect for a little while, with a spate of local, state, and federal reforms. Then our leaders fell back asleep and child-centered education resumed its sway. But the report's warnings are still highly valid. In fact, the causes for worry have intensified, for our scores are lower now than they were in 1983. Here's a picture of the multidecade decline of our recent verbal SAT scores from 1952 to 2012:

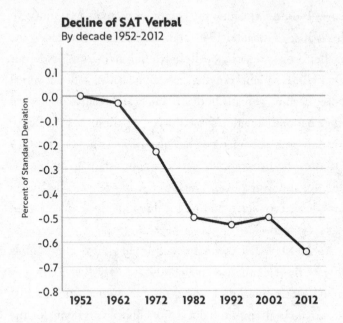

Decline of SAT Verbal
By decade 1952-2012

You can see from the graph that the publication of *A Nation at Risk* in 1983 was followed by a momentary pause in verbal decline—an improvement apparently induced by the report itself. The pause was then followed by a further decline. The 2018 verbal score was *below* that of 2012!

And there's more bad news: The Program of International Student Assessment (PISA) issued its first rankings of reading scores in 2002; at that time, the United States ranked fifteenth in the world in terms of the reading ability of its students. By 2015, we ranked twenty-fourth. The nations that moved ahead of us had taken note from PISA of their shortcomings in schooling, and they improved their results. We continue downward.

Just as a thermometer can indicate indirectly far more than mere temperature, so can a nation's reading-comprehension scores indicate its economic competence and social unity. In the 1930s, 1940s, and 1950s, our students ranked among the top performers internationally in reading and writing. Now our relative international ranking has slipped badly, with our verbal scores declining greatly both absolutely and relative to those of other nations. A nation's reading scores are highly predictive not only of its competence but also of its cohesion, for they indicate whether communication among adults in a nation is effective and widespread. The lower scores reflect a decline in our social, economic, and political competence. We need to make a comeback.

Apologists for our schooling argue that our decline simply reflects the fact that we now "educate everybody," thereby implying that social disadvantage is educational fate; and that our virtuous attempt to educate *all* children accounts for the average decline. There's a small amount of truth in that excuse, but the claim is highly misleading. Social disadvantage is *not* educational fate. Our poor reading scores (and the *very* low verbal scores of our socially disadvantaged students) are mainly artifacts of an incorrect and thoroughly inadequate educational theory held almost universally, alas, in our teacher-training institutions and in our elementary school teaching. We need to fix this urgently.

Here's what we know: For successful communication to take place between an author and a reader, they must share background knowledge. When the people of a nation start sharing more background knowledge, their reading scores improve. *So do their other verbal communications beyond the written word.* A nation's reading scores thus indicate how generally effective other verbal communications are within the nation. When people communicate well, they can work together effectively, learn new things, and gain a sense of community.

Persistently declining reading scores tell us that child-centered education is not working very well for the well-being of our people as a whole. The defects of our child-centered education, stuck in its Romantic ideology, are slowly coming into clear view by scholars and scientists. Change is afoot. We must all hope that it's not too late.

An Example of Shared Knowledge

One scientific insight from recent psychology gets to the heart of what is amiss in encouraging each child to "develop" according to her own inborn nature. We now know some deep-lying mistakes inherent in that view. First, the individual child has no natural inborn developmental blueprint to *be* developed. (Nature wants her to "develop" according to the surrounding culture.) The chief element in that surrounding culture is its shared language. Language mastery is not individual; it's communal. Hence early education is essentially societal, not individualistic. The romantic notion that the individual and the social are inherently part of individual development is a big oversimplification that overlooks the entirely social character of language.

We know that a chief element of language mastery is a vast domain of shared knowledge that is unspoken and unheard. The necessity and extent of this unspoken and unheard dimension of speech—and the need for its common possession among speech participants—is *the* most important finding of language psychology of the past one hundred years.

In retrospect, it seems inevitable that human language evolved to require a large amount of unspoken background knowledge shared silently by members of the tribe. For, in order to communicate nuance of meaning securely and fast, a spoken clause has to be brief. Equally important, it has to be precise in meaning. Brevity and precision in unforeseen circumstances might possibly be accomplished by building a huge vocabulary of subtly different words, each with a precise meaning. But that is far less efficient and flexible than using fewer, more adaptably ambiguous words that are made unambiguous in each circumstance by applying the silently shared background knowledge of the tribe. That is the way human languages and cultures have evolved.

For a child to become a full member of the surrounding society, the child has to learn not what her inborn nature causes her to find interesting, but what others in the society happen to know and take for granted when they communicate in language. Mastery of that background knowledge is the key to effective membership in society. Possession of that silently assumed knowledge is essential for becoming a full member of the surrounding society.

Let's take the simplest possible example—a short nursery rhyme.

> *Polly put the kettle on;*
> *Polly put the kettle on;*
> *Polly put the kettle on;*
> *We'll all have tea.*

These are familiar words, yet it is not possible to understand their meaning accurately unless you already know what "have tea" means, not the two individual words, but the social custom being referred to and what it entails. The other parts of the nursery rhyme aren't self-evident either. Put the kettle on what? What's in the kettle? You need to know that "have tea" implies drinking a drink named "tea," which is made from soaking tea leaves in very hot water. The kettle is needed to heat the water to make the tea.

Water is a very big part of the meaning, though it's not mentioned at all. Neither are cakes and cookies, nor the idea that we will "all" sit down together and chat. The reader or listener must know all those things to understand what "all have tea" means. And it's helpful to understand that you fold up the child's fingers, one by one, in the first stanza and unfold them one by one in the second.

But this is the *American* understanding of "Polly Put the Kettle On." The British understanding has further implications of which democratic Americans are happily innocent. In the British understanding, Polly may *not* be included at the tea table when we "all have tea." She *could* be a daughter of the family (in which case she *would* have tea). But it's more likely that she's a servant and would not be included. In Britain the name "Polly" is a nickname for "Mary," and it's often a generic name for a servant.

Then in the second stanza, the British situation gets even worse in the eyes of an egalitarian American. The stanza goes like this:

Sukie take it off again;
Sukie take it off again;

Sukie take it off again;
They've all gone away.

So there may be at least two servants in this British household. For "Sukie" is similarly a servant-style nickname for "Susan." Thus, the shared knowledge present in each of the two countries will give the children's song subtly different meanings and social ambiguities. The witty Irishman Oscar Wilde observed: "We have really everything in common with America nowadays, except, of course, language." In this case the two languages don't even sound the same. For Americans, "have tea" and "gone away" don't rhyme. But the upper-class British (back when this ditty was composed) did not say *tee* as we do but used the French pronunciation *tay*—which rhymes perfectly with "away."

This trivial example illustrates a far-from-trivial truth about language and human communities. Successful communication in any community depends on commonly shared prior knowledge, which enables all the members of the group to understand the same subtleties of meaning.

The great scholar Karl W. Deutsch wrote a pathbreaking book, *Nationalism and Social Communication* (1953), on the essence of nationhood, which dramatized the point. After enormous descriptive and statistical analysis, he found that the universal essence of unified nationhood is silently shared background knowledge among its citizens. He showed that it isn't a common *language* per se that is at issue. Some successful nations use more than one language. Rather, it's commonly shared, often unspoken background knowledge and values that ultimately enable citizens to understand one another and function effectively. The essence of nationality and ethnicity is what re-searchers have named a "speech community." It is a group of people who share the same meanings in their "social commu-nication" because they share the same unspoken implications, and the same background knowledge.

Now you understand the power of shared knowledge.

CHAPTER 2

The Child-Centered Classroom

This chapter's visit to the elementary classroom is meant to illuminate some realities of the child-centered approach that now governs our early schooling. Looked at from the standpoint of our current knowledge of human psychology, contemporary "child-centered" practice seems like a relic of a strange mass conversion that overcame the well-meaning educational experts of the early twentieth century, whose descendants now teach that misguided gospel to our teachers. An outmoded relic of the past!

But a fair-minded judgment of this anomaly will recognize that the emotional origins of child-centered education are love and affection for young children, along with a faith in natural development that was shared by some of the most advanced thinkers and scientists in the nineteenth and early twentieth centuries. It captured the minds of entire nations in Europe as well as in the United States. But it has left many of our citizens with inadequate educations.

On the international PISA test for fifteen-year-olds, the scores of US children and their relative ranking have both been sinking ever since 2000, when the scores started being recorded.

A fifteen-year-old boy or girl who has not scored well on such a verbal test is not likely to end up being a highly competent person or an informed citizen. The United States has some of the best universities in the world, but they are impossible to get into for many of our young people. That's largely because our child-centered elementary schooling is defective.

To write this chapter, I interviewed Dr. Michele Hudak and Ms. Cathy Kinter, two highly experienced teachers who have each spent half their careers in child-centered elementary classrooms and half in knowledge-centered ones. Ms. Hudak worked in Ohio and in Arizona, and Ms. Kinter in Florida and North Carolina.

In our conversations, the term "standards" was often mentioned. Each state issues its own for elementary school. They are decisive for our public schools and teachers, no matter what the philosophy of the school. But oddly enough, they are devoid of specific content. The problem is that the tenets of child-centered theory insist that these standards *not* be content specific, so that children can choose what they learn according to their individual natures.

Here's an abbreviated list of literacy standards from Ms. Kinter's state of North Carolina:

(Begins in grade 2) L.1.3 (Begins in grade 2) L.2.3 Use knowledge of language and its conventions when writing, speaking, reading, or listening. a. Compare formal and informal uses of English. L.3.3 Use knowledge of language and its conventions when writing, speaking, reading, or listening. a. Choose words and phrases for effect. b. Recognize and observe differences between the conventions of spoken and written standard English. L.4.3 Use knowledge of language and its conventions when writing, speaking, reading, or listening. a. Choose words and phrases to convey ideas precisely. b. Choose punctuation for effect. c. Differentiate between contexts that call for formal English and situations where informal discourse is appropriate. L.5.3 Use knowledge of language and its conventions when writing, speaking, reading, or listening. a. Expand, combine, and reduce sentences for meaning, reader/listener interest, and style. b. Compare and contrast the varieties of English used in stories, dramas, or poems. L.6.3 Use knowledge of language and its conventions when writing, speaking, reading, or listening. a. Vary sentence patterns for meaning, reader/listener interest, and style. b. Maintain consistency in style and tone.

Etc., etc.

I have arranged our discussion under a few basic themes. The first, on standards, has to do less with the child-centered mode of teaching than with the way child-centered ideas have influenced the state authorities who set standards for the elementary years. What children are supposed to learn in common are merely general acquisitions like "language proficiency" and "critical thinking" skills. As we will discover from the interviews, this means that the real determiners of the curriculum tend to be the individual teachers themselves in their individual classrooms, for better and for worse.

Another essential characteristic of the early grades in our schools is the current *physical* setup of the elementary classroom. One of the striking changes that child-centered education introduced was to remove the individual small desks all facing the front of the room. These were replaced by four or five tables, set inside the perimeter, with a rug often in the middle or on the side with cushions or beanbag seats. At these tables four or five young students sit facing not the teacher but one another. This innovation is so universal now in the United States that it usually characterizes both the child-centered and the knowledge-centered classroom. In the child-centered classroom, these tables sometimes serve as "centers." And the children around the tables are called "groups."

Standards That Aren't Standards

MICHELE: I think in science there was one directive that said I needed to teach the three states of matter—solids, liquids, and gasses—but that was it. No further instructions. Teach the three states of matter. So I decided that I was going to teach a unit on bubbles. I'm not really sure why. I mean, bubbles are gasses I guess, but that's what my colleagues were doing, so I taught a unit on bubbles, and we blew bubbles, and we talked about a bubble of gas, and I grabbed a couple of solids.

So it was very disjointed. I mean, I don't know how else to say it: it was very disjointed. And even apples. You know, I think we had to teach the four seasons. So I thought, "Well, the best way to teach the four seasons is to teach a unit on apples, because I can just go through the seasonal cycles of an apple tree."

E. D. HIRSCH: That raises another quick question, I don't want to interrupt too much, but is that, would you say, typical of districts across the country, that you're given only this really very general guidance about content?

MICHELE: Yes, yes. I told my own children I was going to teach in a new [knowledge-centered] school, where we knew in advance exactly the things the children had already learned, and we also knew what we needed to teach this year, so I said to my kids: "Listen, Mom's going to go to this knowledge-based school." And even my daughter said, "Well, that's a good thing, Mom."

EDH: I can't get my mind around the idea of so little guidance for teachers.

MICHELE: Well, my daughter said, "Mom, I think I'm going to come to *your* school." And I said, "Why? You don't have to," and she said, "Mom, every year, in science, since I was in kindergarten, I learned about plants. I've had the same packets on plants since I was in first grade." And she said, "I'm just tired of plants. So I think I want to go to your school to learn something else."

———

CATHY: The way that I met those standards was left up to me. I may have a particular textbook that I would begin and then go through the whole year, or I may not. So—

EDH: That raises another question.

CATHY: Yes.

EDH: Do you mean that normally in what you're calling the child-centered classrooms, that the teacher will choose his or her own materials and textbooks to meet these very general standards?

CATHY: Yes. I think back to when I first went to North Carolina and I taught science in fifth grade. I had a set of North Carolina "standards," but I did not have any kind of curriculum or anything. It had no content. Think like a scientist and so on. Here are your standards, how you meet them is completely and totally up to you.

EDH: So you're looking at that issue from both angles, as a teacher and a mother?

CATHY: Yes. But the way that I met those standards oftentimes was left up to me. I rummaged around to select my own materials.

Not Content, but "Skills"

EDH: So the standards were never content standards?

CATHY: No.

EDH: They were what?

CATHY: Reading standards, math standards, writing standards.

EDH: They were skill standards, were they?

CATHY: Yes, yes. Very skills based.

EDH: I see, okay. Now I'm getting the picture.

The Child-Centered Centers

Another principle of the child-centered classroom is that children learn best when they help construct their own knowledge. From the standpoint of pedagogy, this is probably the idea that most distinguishes child-centered education. It's what changed the configuration of the classroom from desks facing the teacher to large tables where the children face one another. Knowledge that arises from their own active *inquiry*, or *problem solving*, or *exploring*, or *questioning*, or *discovering* is said to be more firmly fixed in the mind than mere information that a child passively receives from a teacher's lecturing. Young teachers-to-be are told: "Don't be a sage on the stage. Be a guide on the side."

MICHELE: Another child-centered idea when I was teaching first grade was that idea of centers—work centers for students, right? You put these centers in place so that children could explore. There were literacy and math centers, so I had this 180-minute block. That's a lot of minutes for a young child to be exploring. I don't even think I wrote lesson plans the first three years that I was a child-centered teacher, because I spent all this time creating these independent work centers with the kids.

And so they moved from one center to another and I had a bell and after fifteen minutes I would ding it and they would move to the next one. After five minutes they were done, and there was usually mass chaos ensuing, so then I would have to create more centers because I knew that the kids could maintain attention for only five to seven minutes. So there I was on the weekends at school, creating twenty-five centers. I had this graph of a movement system to get the kids to move through, and then at the end of the day I would be exhausted.

And you know there was no depth to any of it. You know, we'd say, "Let's make words." Well, how does a child make words when a child doesn't know how to read? And I was saying to myself, "There just has to be an easier way," but I was too young in the profession. You know, we were coming through those days of "invented spelling" [in which] it doesn't matter how they spell, because someday they will get it.

I tried to teach my standards through their interests. So my guided reading centers might be like this: In this center we were building words about spiders. In this center we were reading a reading passage and answering questions about butterflies. In this center we were watching a video. In this center, which was my guided reading center, I might have leveled texts [books at different levels of challenge] about spiders.

EDH: Cathy, could you say a little bit about centers. What was the idea of these centers and how did they actually work?

CATHY: The idea behind the centers was that you were able to differentiate, to meet students where they were and to take them as far as they could.

EDH: What does a center actually look like?

CATHY: It could look different in different classrooms. A center, basically, is a small group of students working on an activity together. Oftentimes they were student generated, in that there would not be a teacher working with them. To meet the needs of students, you couldn't give them whole-group instruction. So you broke it down into small, manageable groups, with hopefully pretty high-interest activities so students would maintain engagement throughout them, even though you were not right there watching them.

[*Author's note:* There *could* not be a whole-class discussion, because the background knowledge of each child was so unpredictably different, largely because their prior classes had been on different individualized topics. Hence, there was no possibility of a successful speech community in the class.]

EDH: In a way, they were teaching themselves at these centers.

CATHY: Correct, yes.

EDH: Because the teacher couldn't deal with the whole class, because there was such varied background among the students?

CATHY: Correct. The teacher was usually at the reading center, where students were reading leveled books. So you were working on reading skills and comprehension while the other students were working on different tasks related to a standard, but again, hopefully high-interest enough that it was engaging to them and it would maintain their attention for fifteen minutes. And then they would switch.

EDH: How did you prepare? You're preparing for the class to come in, and so how do you prepare who goes where and, physically, what do the centers look like?

CATHY: It took a lot of preparation time. I would make games or find videos. At one point in my classroom I was lucky that we had [a place] where kids could watch a video and then I could create questions right after the video and they could record their responses to the questions. There would be a file folder of games.

EDH: So how many centers would there typically be?

CATHY: Most of the time it would depend on how many students you had in your classroom, because I always wanted somebody to have a partner. The idea of the centers is to generate some student involvement with each other. So if I was teaching twenty-five students, you really never wanted more than five. It could be anywhere, honestly, from four to six centers that I had going in my classroom at the same time.

EDH: So, a lot of this, the interaction between the students, would be students teaching themselves. Have I got the picture right? Since it's not teacher directed.

CATHY: No, it's not teacher directed. . . . There are times I would have a listening station where they would put headphones on and follow along with a book. Or there would be books about [specific] topics. We just didn't know what kind of conversations were happening over there in the centers. I was hoping for the most part that they were talking about the text that they were supposed to be reading or they were pulling some meaning from it. As long as they did not attract undue attention by being completely off task, that allowed me to work with my students at my current small group.

EDH: I see.

CATHY: Kind of terrible, huh?

Incoherence and Unshared Knowledge

CATHY: There was a lot of variation among the classes. We had five third-grade classrooms. You're now looking at 125 kids coming from every classroom with hopefully the same "standards-based" education, but not any kind of specific content. I could have taught those standards through an exploration of astronomy, or the rain forest, and my fellow teacher might have taught the same standards through a completely different subject matter—a novel or an old textbook or something she found from a secondhand exchange.

EDH: So different classrooms at the same grade level in the same school are teaching different content?

CATHY: Correct. There was no shared content at all.

The next day, maybe they were interested in Blackbeard. So we were studying Blackbeard. It was connected through the day but it wasn't connected day-to-day.

Critical Thinking about Nothing in Particular

EDH: You're a guide on the side.

MICHELE: Yes. You know, the idea was if you want kids to think critically you need to let them solve their own problems, and I guess my argument to that is, give kids rich curriculum and let them ask questions about it, and there's your so-called critical thinking.

EDH: On that point, did you actually spend time on critical thinking as a process?

MICHELE: Yes, I would have critical thinking packets that

I gave my kids, but I didn't see that it made any difference.

EDH: Let us go into that just a little bit more, if you don't mind, because I'm interested in how much time was spent on your critical thinking packets, and what is a critical thinking packet.

MICHELE: Sometimes I had to make it up. A lot of times I would go to Barnes and Noble, which had a teacher's section, so this was before the internet was widely used. I would find a little reproducible book that would say "Critical Thinking." There would be things like analogies and logic puzzles, not content but things of a puzzle-type nature. I would buy it, copy it, put it in a packet, and then I would say to the kids who were way beyond what I was teaching that day in say, mathematics, to use their stapled packets. They would engage in something completely different from the math I was teaching that day.

What I found later on is that in a knowledge-based school, children don't have a lot of extra time to waste on so-called critical-thinking tasks. Every instructional minute matters because we have so much content to deliver. In a typical child-centered school, teachers will put these critical-thinking packets together for kids because they have more time on their hands.

At my current knowledge-based school, we just don't have any time on our hands for critical-thinking packets, because every subject carries equal weight. In a knowledge-based school, you are reading, you are writing, you are talking, in every subject area.

Child-Centered Civics

EDH: But look, if you're studying expanding horizons, is everybody studying the same neighborhood and then the same town and the same state and then the same . . . I mean, is it actually some of the content overlapping in the different classrooms?

CATHY: I would imagine some of it is, because when you're thinking about student-centered, you are hitting the students where they are. So we would be studying the same town, the same state, that type of thing.

On the other hand, when you are also thinking about student-centered, if you have students or a student who moved in new to the state or, oftentimes, moved in from Mexico, it could be expanded as well, because you're thinking about the interest of the student.

EDH: It was the expanding-horizons kind of idea?

CATHY: Yes.

EDH: So from the small group to the neighborhood, then to the city and then to the country, that sort of thing?

CATHY: Yes, correct.

EDH: Expanding horizons didn't give them a lot of history, did it?

CATHY: No, no, not at all.

MICHELE: The social studies standards are such that they learn only the same old stuff: about themselves, their home, and their community.

EDH: Oh, my goodness.

MICHELE: And literacy, you know, in my child-centered days I had the 180-minute uninterrupted literacy block. I had just a half hour a day to teach history, science, and geography. Mind you those so-called child-centered materials were in the form of worksheets or little projects. Let's make a teepee or a totem pole to study Native Americans, and they could take their little packets of papers home. There was little to no content. And I can tell you as an educator I didn't even know where to go to look for content. But really it didn't matter, because you teach the big three and that's really where you spend the bulk of your time.

EDH: By big three you mean reading, writing, and arithmetic?

MICHELE: Yes. Going back to my days in a child-centered school, we did something called project-based learning in my first years. We had to create an authentic problem for students to solve in their community. So my colleagues and I in first grade got together and we came up with a problem. We pretended the local park was going to be closed, and we had to generate a letter-writing campaign to try to keep the park open and provide reasons why the park should remain open.

And so those poor children really believed that they were closing one of their local parks, because we had to make it authentic. And there had to have been some kind of ecology tied to it, I don't know—maybe people were littering or something. But what can first graders do? They're learning how to write, and we're going to have them write a letter. It was just so artificial. They could see through it. They might not know how to write, but they were smart.

And then my colleague in second grade, her project was about how to choose the best class pet. So again, there was very little content to tie it to, and really, as the kids were diving into it, we would get books on ecology and things for the children to explore, but they were really prompted to make their own meaning and solve the problem, so to speak, in the best way that they knew how. So we did that for maybe a year, without much forward progress, and that kind of went by the wayside as well, because again, I don't know that we were getting any bang for our buck.

Personalization and Differentiation

EDH: It seems that the so-called child-centered school ends up being a kind of routine affair. I don't quite get it, because the theory and rhetoric of the child-centered school is that learning has to be personalized.

MICHELE: In my early years at a knowledge-centered school, I tried to differentiate instruction for the students who were identified as gifted. For example, when we studied astronomy, I had a lot of gifted students who had a passion for astronomy, and so I would set up a web quest for them. They already knew the information that I had to share because they were pretty passionate about it, and so I set them up in the back to just continue to further their knowledge. Within two days, the kids came back to the larger group. They wanted to be a part of the great conversation. They wanted to share their knowledge with their fellow students. They didn't want to sit there and necessarily learn more about astronomy. They wanted to have a conversation about it.

EDH: What about the differentiation of abilities in the two kinds of schools? In the so-called child-centered school, was there more differentiation of instruction and topic?

MICHELE: Yes. I'm not opposed to the theory of differentiation, because there are children who need more assistance. But what I found is, we were told to differentiate for the sake of differentiating.

EDH: That boggles my mind. It was done independent of the particular needs of the kids?

MICHELE: Yes, the idea was that if differentiation is a good thing, do it for all kids.

EDH: Wait a minute. I'm a little confused. I thought differentiation meant you differed the instruction when needed for different kids.

MICHELE: In my experience it was, "We're going to differentiate for kids because it's good for kids, so make sure in your lesson plans that you always have a plan for differentiation." When educational ideas come forth such as personalized learning or differentiation, I think what happens is that educators or school districts jump on the bandwagon. They give a little bit of training and then say, "Now do it." In the knowledge-based school, it's, "We will do it if there's a need." And what we've found is, when you have a strong knowledge-based curriculum, the need for special help is no longer as great.

Michele on the Contrast between Child-Centered and Knowledge-Centered Schools

MICHELE: My son Ethan attended a knowledge-centered school, and it was the end of third grade. My husband and I were out to dinner with him one night and my husband said, "So Ethan. What was your favorite subject in school this year?" And he said Rome. And he began with the story of Romulus and Remus, and I'm not exaggerating when I tell you that for one hour we sat and listened to him recite the rise and fall of the Roman Empire in detail.

Ethan was in the first class of eighth graders that experienced a knowledge-based school all the way through elementary school. They were our test group. They are all freshman in college now, and their awards and scholarships and accolades and university choices are just unbelievable.

EDH: We know what the end product is. You've just described it—college for all. But how would you describe the difference in what is actually going on in child-centered and knowledge-centered classrooms?

MICHELE: Okay. I'll give you a good example. In my daughter's third-grade child-centered classroom, they were given a basic reader. Some of the stories are excerpts of classic literature and other stories are just stories that a publisher makes up and puts in an anthology.

You come to a knowledge-based classroom, and the students begin their day with the Vikings. During reading we are exploring the Viking myths and having a rich discussion about that. We go to the domain-based read-alouds and we're now reading aloud about the Vikings.

Everybody feels they're *getting* somewhere from one day to the next. And they are using sophisticated tier-three words in conversation!

EDH: Would you say the kids are more engaged?

MICHELE: Oh my gosh, they love it. My husband and I used to joke with our own kids. They'd come home from school, and we would say at the dinner table, "What did you learn today?" And they would say, "Nothing." And my husband would then say to them, "Well, then don't go back."

And then once they got to a knowledge-centered school we'd say, "What did you learn in science today," or "What did you learn in history and geography?" And they talked and talked about it. Those are the conversations that the kids themselves are having. And I will tell you, the parents of our knowledge-centered school will say to me, "You know, Dr. Hudak, I cannot get over, my son and my daughter come home and they are excited about school." When kids come back after the summer, they can't wait to come back to school. There's not this dull "Oh gosh we're here again and we're filling out packets of worksheets again."

Another huge contrast is that in a knowledge-based school, when you have children engaged in content, you need time. We don't have enough time to get all the information to the kids. So to get through it you're moving pretty quickly. But the benefit of moving pretty quickly is that you have less difficulty with behavior because the kids are so engaged in what they are learning. Kids who are supposed to be naughty coming to me are absolutely fine. Why? Because they are engaged.

These school districts are looking for silver bullets to end the achievement gap, but really, it's not that hard. Even our neediest kids are now freshmen in college. These were kids that came through my third-grade classroom, struggling students. But by the time they got to eighth grade they weren't struggling anymore. They were products of a great curriculum. They were hard workers. Their parents supported the movement. They struggled. And they're walking out successful.

When you have something that is coherent, cumulative, sequenced, something that kids could tie knowledge onto, it makes for a much more successful experience for struggling kids. When you look at the vocabulary that these kids are getting, tier one, tier two, and tier three, especially our tier-two vocabulary, these are rich, rich classrooms.

Cathy on the Contrast between Child-Centered and Knowledge-Centered Schools

CATHY: I spent fourteen years in what I would consider to be a more child-centered classroom, in which I was a primary teacher from preschool to sixth grade. I like to refer to the child-centered classroom as pocketed, isolated learning. We'd do one thing, then we would go to a different thing. The subjects weren't connected. So we did our best. We'd have our standards, and we'd follow guidelines set by the school district.

EDH: Tell me something about the difference between the two kinds of schools.

CATHY: I wouldn't even know where to start. I will tell you my first memory of being a parent and completely being overwhelmed with emotion by what my child was getting at the knowledge-based school. I had a sixth-grade student who was in a child-centered school, and I had a first grader who was at a knowledge-based school. We were having dinner at the dinner table, and I remember this like it was yesterday.

As most parents do, we said to the first grader, "So what'd you learn in school today?" And she said, "Mama, we're talking about Mesopotamia." Out of my peripheral vision I could see my sixth grader at the end of the table with her eyes wide open. My first grader continues to go on about how they're learning about cuneiform and how Mesopotamia's considered the cradle of civilization because every civilization since then etc., etc. She's going on and on. And I remember Taylor, my sixth grader, putting her hands down on the table, and saying, "Mesapawhat? Mama, I'm in sixth grade and I've never heard of Mesopotamia." My husband and I made eye contact, and I just said, "See? See? This is why we made the change we made."

This epitomizes the difference in the education they had. Taylor was the proverbial oldest child. We read to her every night. She had all the advantages. The other four came boom, boom, boom. I was in grad school, so we were busy. We didn't read every night. We didn't do everything we were supposed to do. But despite that, those later kids flourished in their knowledge-based primary and middle schools in a way that absolutely changed our family dynamics. Instead of going to the beach every summer, we would go places like Ellis Island or Washington, DC. Yes. I know that might sound goody-goody, but they wanted to do it.

From a parental perspective, you couldn't give me enough time to speak about the difference in education it makes having a shared body of knowledge that builds up over time. When they're in the younger grades, they grow this small seed of knowledge, and then as it's continued; it cycles up and you're adding to it. It becomes that whole association and assimilation idea that I learned about in undergrad but was never truly able to help my students gain access to. I knew they had it in their minds somewhere, but they were never able to find it, because they had lots of little seeds, but nothing built up to a wider scheme of knowledge they could access and add to.

I see that that's what a coherent knowledge-based school does. Students can retrieve and connect things. As teachers, we're not having to guess about their prior experiences. We can absolutely tap into those prior experiences and we can help them access them.

In the past, at a child-centered school, it was like, "Do you remember that?" "No." But now we can specifically say to a fifth-grade student, "All right, so do you remember when you were in second grade and you learned about President Lincoln's desire to keep the Union together?" And they all say, "Yes!" So we, as teachers, are empowered to be able to specifically tap into that important resource that helps students build their knowledge forward.

EDH: It seems to me that if I can interpret what you are saying, our memories are connected to specific knowledge. To build on past learnings, and even to communicate with the class, you need common reference points. If you can depend on the class having some common background knowledge, then your communications with *all* the students are better understood.

CATHY: Absolutely. The way that I would compare the two is this: child-centered schools tend to be more compartmentalized. We take our students on day one and we go as far as we can with them until day 180. But everything is kind of disconnected and self-contained, and it's different from student to student. Math did not connect to science, which did not connect to history or to language arts.

EDH: I take it in your child-centered days, when you received students from somebody else's class, you couldn't depend on all the students knowing the same things, could you?

CATHY: No. I couldn't depend on students knowing *anything*. Here in Charlotte in the child-centered county school, we had five second-grade classrooms, and I was teaching third and fourth grade.

On day one of third grade, my second graders would come in with all different kinds of content knowledge. It was standards based, so *theoretically* they should be coming in with the same standards. But the way that they got to those standards could have been any subject matter whatsoever. It's much harder to make significant progress with those students.

EDH: What's going on now that you're teaching in a knowledge-based school?

CATHY: I'm now an instructional coach for a beginning knowledge-based school in a very high poverty situation. Some of our kids are homeless, some of them live in a hotel. It's a very sad situation. This school is now currently in its fifth year, and we are starting to see remarkable progress.

It has been hard, because the teachers have to go through a lot of change in mind-set to move from a child-centered curriculum to a knowledge-centered one. But now, for the first time in its history, this high-poverty school has moved way up in the rankings. And that's great, but that's not what it's all about.

What it's all about is being in those hallways and hearing the kids saying, "Oh, I remember learning that in first grade," and their being able to build from there. And watching them in sixth grade talking about the Mayans that they learned about in fifth grade. So, you're seeing a change in school culture. The children are *so* excited!

EDH: It seems to me that at the same time that a teacher can depend on certain background knowledge, the students are themselves making more of a community among themselves because they share some of the same background knowledge from the previous grade levels. So it would stand to reason that a kind of culture and unity would develop in the student body itself. Is that what you're telling me?

CATHY: Absolutely, and it extends outside the student body, too, because that culture starts to develop in the families of those students as well. Just as our own family vacations changed, I watched that happen with the families in our own schools. We're very close to Myrtle Beach, so everybody always goes to the beach over the summer. But as our schools started becoming knowledge based, the vacation pattern changed. Students are starting to come in with pictures from their tour out west, because they wanted to go see the Oregon Trail, or going to Ellis Island and other places they've learned about. And, mind you, these are regular public school kids.

A third-grade class at one of the knowledge-centered schools I oversee here in North Carolina is in the middle of studying animal classification. On a recent visit I stepped back and took myself out of the conversation. The teachers had been teaching a long time in child-centered schools, one for fourteen years, the other for twenty plus. They were both talking about how this is the first time in their teaching career that students are so excited about what they're learning that they're checking books out of the public library. One student brought a snakeskin in, another an alligator necklace that someone gave him.

The school itself is becoming a community. They all have a lot they can share. They have all this knowledge now, and these kids are learning how to access it outside of school. That's so exciting.

EDH: Any final thoughts?

CATHY: I always try to tell skeptical parents and teachers this: "Think about the ranges of students that you have in your classroom who all are being excited by this content. And because that content is so engaging, think how much easier it is to use this content to narrow those gaps and extend students even further. You can do so much more in terms of writing when you put second graders in an authentic situation where they're writing a persuasive letter to President Lincoln from the perspective of an abolitionist.

"Think of how you can get your students to understand, and be more empathetic about our immigration situation today when they have gained knowledge from the immigration history that they learned in second grade."

For me, I don't know that I would still be doing this if I did not move to a knowledge-based classroom, because I was so frustrated. In 2007, when I was able to move and could teach something besides reading skills and math skills, I said to myself, "Oh my gosh, this is why I came into teaching."

EDH: I wanted to ask you one other thing. There's a subtle decline of patriotism in the country that Gallup poll keeps recognizing every year, and I'm wondering whether this sort of communitarian approach encourages allegiance, the idea that we're all in this together and need to make our country better.

CATHY: From my perspective, the two things are connected. In a knowledge-based school, the students in the music room are practicing the "Star-Spangled Banner"; in another classroom they are studying the American Revolution—so many opportunities to develop citizenship thinking beyond the school community. Again, you've got that shared body of knowledge. I see more singing in the knowledge-based school. I see more general school-wide assemblies where students are talking about current events or talking about our national heroes of all races and backgrounds.

EDH: Absolutely. The original common school idea that "you kids are the upcoming citizens, you will define the country" was paramount in those early days. Also the idea that the more unified we get, the more competent we get, because the more you can communicate with one another, the more competent the country gets.

CATHY: Absolutely. In the child-centered school, everything is so isolated and compartmentalized. I recognize for the most part there are really good teachers out there and they're working really, really, really hard. But when you are so focused on what I have to teach my fourth graders, for them to show proficiency on the end-of-grade test, skills become your focus.

But when you are focused on the shared curriculum, your perspective really opens up. As a teacher, it puts us back where many teachers were when education was more successful, and we looked at the student in a much broader sense as a future citizen, and not just, "I've got to get this kid to pass a test at the end of the year."

EDH: It makes sense to me. Absolutely.

CHAPTER 3

"Nobody Leaves"

The Dazzling Success of Shared-Knowledge Schools

*One morning, I was on the playground before school supervising the students'
play. Makayla, a second-grade student, came running up to me, shouting,
"I'm so excited for today!" I asked, "Why is that?" I expected her to say
that it was her birthday or some other special event. But she exclaimed,
"Because today we are going to learn about the War of 1812!" I said,
"Gee, I wonder what that is about?" "I don't know," she said. "But today
I'm going to find out!"*

—Ms. Lari Nelson, principal of a [core knowledge]
regular public school in Riverside, California

There are numerous examples of what our schooling can
be—in both regular public schools and charter schools.
Never mind those labels! A good school is a good school. I want
to share some real-world examples (which could be multiplied
currently by hundreds of others) to bring the war of ideas about
the aims and methods of our elementary schools to life.

Teachers and parents especially need to be liberated from
the doctrines of child-centered education—a liberation that

is all the more urgent given the power of the brilliant slogans that have captured the minds of young future teachers in our schools of education. Who can resist "A teacher should be a guide on the side, not a sage on the stage" or "One size does not fit all," among other rhetorically effective terms and phrases that claim to have firm scientific backing? Who would even wish to resist such slogans when we are told that the alternative to a child-centered approach is mindless rote learning and boredom?

A lot of such negative characterizations *are* true of poor teaching under any theory! And of course, the child-centered advocates are right that every child is unique. Every elementary school is unique: the teachers are unique, as are the students, the building, the general atmosphere. But some schools are objectively a lot better than others. They have happy, eager students who feel strongly attached to the school community. They are fond of their teachers and their peers, and they are learning a lot. And even those students whose caregivers are poor and semiliterate slowly begin to catch up with their more advantaged classmates.

There is only one *kind* of school that accomplishes that double goal of quality and equality. It is the shared-knowledge school. Such a school transforms each classroom into a speech community. By means of shared prior lessons, all the students in each classroom possess the key background knowledge that will enable them to understand the new lesson. This principle of preparatory sequencing has always been applied in mathematics instruction. But the principle should apply to *every* subject, because all genuine learning requires the possession of shared, unspoken knowledge that enables accurate comprehension. This simple fact explains the unique effectiveness of the shared-knowledge school.

Currently, the child-centered school is more prevalent in the United States. There are tens of thousands of child-centered public schools exhibiting various degrees of individualized subject matter in the language arts. Across the nation, there are fewer than five thousand shared-knowledge public schools. Thirty years ago, there were none.

Just a Regular Public School

My first example of an American school success is a regular public school in my state of Virginia: the Lyles-Crouch Traditional Academy in Alexandria. Its student body is racially, ethnically, and economically diverse, multilingual, and of different abilities. Yet all its students reach a high level of achievement. It is the highest-scoring school in the district. The students love it. The parents love it. The superintendent has voted with his feet: he has moved to the neighborhood so his third grader can attend this particular school.

Lyles-Crouch elementary has no special financial advantages. It's just as underfinanced as the other schools in the district. Located in a mixed-income neighborhood, the school must endure all the disadvantages that public school leaders often cite to excuse poor educational performance: that they are underfinanced, that they must accept students from all circumstances, that charter schools cream the best students from the top and exclude low performers, that regular schools must follow onerous rules, that the home culture of students is antilearning, and so on. All those drawbacks apply to Lyles-Crouch.

How Lyles-Crouch Transformed Itself

After the 1970s, with the ending of school segregation in Virginia, Lyles-Crouch became a de facto segregated all-black school. White families fled the area or placed their children elsewhere. Its enrollment fell to 110 students. Despite that low enrollment, in 2004, a veteran principal, Dr. Patricia Zissios, was selected to lead the school. She had come to question the validity of the child-centered principles that had been handicapping students in her prior schools, and she became determined to introduce a shared-knowledge approach with a strong civic and ethical orientation.

She persuaded her staff that instead of focusing attention on the individual characteristics of the child and offering students a wide choice of helter-skelter readings in language arts from the classroom library or from please-everyone textbooks, they should use a new mode whereby each grade would learn common subject matter month by month. Knowledge was to build on knowledge cumulatively. A schoolwide approach to the subject matter of each grade would ensure over time that no child would be left behind.

"But, how then will individual differences be accommodated?" asked her constructivist-indoctrinated teachers. ("Constructivism" encourages the individual child to "construct" her own education, based on her own instincts and powers.) I asked Dr. Zissios the same question. Here's her answer:

> We use the timing of subjects being taught as a framework, not as scripted, lockstep instruction. Teachers present the subject matter through a variety of means to meet the needs of all of our students. We use multiple-leveled books,

technology, community resources, field experiences, and so on to extend, enrich, and expand the common subject matter. Abler students do independent projects and research. We tailor the instruction within the individual class to promote appropriate learning for each student. Learning the same subject matter does not equate to learning it in the same way or at the same level or at the exact same time.

Yet even with this accommodating approach, the same subject matter does get learned in the same week and month, so that each child in each grade of the Lyles-Crouch school moves forward in a productive way—not in exactly the same way and with the same velocity, but covering the same topics: photosynthesis, the Bill of Rights, the Civil War. No child is left with gaping holes in his or her knowledge. And this common knowledge becomes the enabling foundation for further shared knowledge in the following month or grade level. It's not a complex pedagogical idea, and it's been well tested.

A Recent Study

Here's a quick glimpse of how shared knowledge has been tested scientifically. There are currently some two thousand core knowledge elementary schools, including regular public schools, charter schools, and private schools. These elementary schools and other programs that follow the common-content principle are far outperforming their neighboring schools— and I can now tell you by how much on average. A recent multischool study in Colorado by Professor David Grissmer, a well-regarded researcher at the University of Virginia, compares the progress of students from first through third grade, with half the children randomly assigned to child-centered schools with personalized curricula, and half with a specific core knowledge curriculum for all the children in the class.

Professor Grissmer drew from a pool of some 1,400 Colorado first graders, whose parents wanted them to attend one of the 120 core knowledge schools in Colorado. That was too many first graders for too few schools, so a lottery had to be arranged. There were places for about half the kids. The unlucky other half were left to attend the local district child-centered schools.

All the students in the pool thus had solicitous parents, eliminating the neglectful parent as an element that might distort the results. After three years, Dr. Grissmer reported a verbal-achievement difference between the two groups of more than half a standard deviation favoring the knowledge-centered schools, *and a difference among the most disadvantaged students of two-thirds of a standard deviation!* These are decisive results.

Lyles-Crouch . . . Continued

Teaching everyone the same topic is a not a complex idea, but it is a brave, heretical one for a principal to advocate in the current intellectual context of American schools. Dr. Zissios demonstrated great courage in disobeying the doctrines set forth by her then superintendent, who cautioned against "lock-step" education, and urged teachers to develop their students' "critical thinking skills" and "reading comprehension skills," just as teachers at most other American schools are urged to do. Dr. Zissios's new policy constituted a brave, job-threatening apostasy.

But Dr. Zissios did persuade her teachers to try the new idea. Her school introduced common grade-by-grade content for all. Morale at Lyles-Crouch rose among both students and teachers. Every child was now more or less on the same page, learning a great many interesting things, and feeling a sense of empowerment and fellowship. The gap between advantaged and disadvantaged students diminished. Everybody was having a good time. The atmosphere at Lyles-Crouch became electric with enthusiasm.

Other local parents with children in expensive private schools heard about the new energy and the new approach of focusing on content rather than practicing skills. Enrollment increased every year—from 110 students in 2004 to 441 as of 2020. The student population is now bursting out of its building, and the school cannot accept more students.

Soon the test scores at Lyles-Crouch rose above those of all other elementary schools in Alexandria, including schools in much more prosperous neighborhoods. It was a remarkable transformation. As Dr. Zissios emailed me in answer to my inquiry:

Over the last three school years, we have outperformed all other schools in the Alexandria City Public Schools. We have had all scores in the 90th percentile or above. (In fact, in history, we achieved 99%; one student failed the exam.) Because of our excellent passing rates, over the last ten years, we have been awarded the Virginia Board of Education's Distinguished Achievement Award (2007–2010; 2012–2016) and Virginia Board of Education's Award of Excellence (2010–2011, 2016–2017). We have been recognized as a Best School in 2012 and named Top School for 2017 by *Northern Virginia* magazine. Our current scores put us in the top 5% of the entire Commonwealth of Virginia for academic achievement.

What about the socioeconomic character of the school? Dr. Zissios wrote:

Today, we have 441 students, 10% ELL [English Language Learners] (mainly Ethiopians speaking Amharic), 10% special education (with citywide autism class), and 28% living in poverty. We are 55% white, 30% black, 5% Asian/Pacific Islander, 7% Hispanic, & 3% other. Our mobility rate is 20% due to military families and state department personnel living in our attendance zone.

This socioeconomic diversity and transience (one-fifth of Lyles-Crouch's students come and go each year) is true of many public schools around the world. It's a technical handicap, but one that can be overcome by a well-thought-out curriculum that prepares all students in the district for the next step in learning. Moreover, as a nation's elementary schools become more effective, and the parents of the nation become more literate and knowledgeable, the next generation will enter school better prepared.

Why haven't all schools in Alexandria gotten the message? I asked Dr. Zissios: Did her school's example have any effect on the surrounding schools of the district? This is her emailed answer, which has significant implications for parents and policy makers across the land:

I have found it quite fascinating that our performance year after year puts us at the top of the district, and yet no other school embraces knowledge-based learning. We have local community support. We have been acknowledged by several members of the Alexandria City community at large (including the current Mayor) as being a school to be emulated. Even members of the current Alexandria City Public Schools School Board have admitted that Lyles-Crouch must be doing something right to consistently perform as well as we do. We have not been able to get Central Office administrators (i.e., Superintendent, Chief Academic Officer, Director of Elementary Programs) to try it at other sites. I have offered out my staff and school to help others in the district try it at their schools. No one has taken me up on my offer.

The basic reason that no one has taken up her offer is that the dominant child-centered idea has been so well indoctrinated in teachers-to-be by our education schools that child-centeredness has wielded an intellectual monopoly. No nefarious motive is needed to explain why "individually appropriate" topics and discovery learning and other naturalistic ideas get almost religious adherence.

Against the Demographic Odds in the South Bronx

Let's now turn to another version of the same story, but in a sociological world distant from Alexandria, Virginia. The schools are located in the low-income South Bronx, New York City. The Bronx is the poorest, most disadvantaged borough in New

York City, with the highest poverty rate: 30 percent, scoring 10 percentage points worse than the city average. Schools with high poverty rates and large numbers of minority students typically perform badly on standardized tests, and those in the South Bronx fit this pattern overall. But there are exceptions. A few schools have enthusiastic pupils and teachers, and score high on standardized tests. These have been honored by New York State as "Reward Schools." A remarkable percentage of these schools are core knowledge schools overseen by a hero of American education, Jeff Litt. These core knowledge schools are called "Icahn Schools," because the philanthropist Carl Icahn provided the funds for the buildings. But Jeff runs these schools solely with the public funds received by all the public schools in New York City.

The New York State Department of Education defines Reward Schools as "schools with high academic achievement or those with the most progress in the State, and [are schools that] *do not have significant gaps in student achievement between subgroups*." Of the 244 regular public grade schools in the Bronx, two regular schools received recognition as a Reward School, a school that had improved learning for all, and narrowed the gaps among racial, ethnic, and economic groups. And of these two regular public schools, only one achieved an above-average score for low-income students: PS 69 in District 10. That's one-half of one percent of the South Bronx schools. I sought to find out what PS 69 was up to.

After a couple of phone chats with Ms. Sheila Durant, the busy principal of PS 69, I discovered that getting such results in a big school district requires complex political talents. The realities: You have multiple constituencies, and you have to be a savvy politician whose inherent niceness comes across. You have only low-income students, of every color, creed, and national origin. Parents love you because the children are getting great results; your teachers love you because decisions are made by consensus and cooperation, creating a positive communal atmosphere. But steely firmness is also required.

Once community decisions are made, everyone has to get on board in PS 69. When I asked Ms. Durant how she accounted for the remarkable test scores her school achieved, her answer was, "It's the culture of the school. Everybody is on the same page." The need to honor everyone's home culture among the hugely diverse student body is reinforced on a daily basis. Teachers may vary their means of instruction with individual students, but they use the same books and topics in each classroom. "Our curriculum is unified both vertically [across the different grade levels] and horizontally [across different classrooms within the same grade]." Very subtly, and with lots of emphasis on sensitivity to all cultures, the term "literacy" is used as a neutral term to mean "Americanization" and the need for a shared print culture. Each child in the school has received individual encouragement and acknowledgment of her home culture—but all are receiving the same "literacy" and "school culture" as the other students, including its chief moral and social precept ("Be kind to everyone").

It's a shared-knowledge school, in a relaxed way. The emphasis on cultural diversity and empathetic interaction with each pupil is accompanied by an insistence on giving the same "literacy" to all. The theme of diversity is itself made the agent of unity. And the unifying "literacy" component—which includes the "cultural literacy" element—prepares the students for the next class and the next, and for the next year. Shared knowledge at work!

————

Then there are the charter schools of the South Bronx. Their percentages for achieving Reward status are a bit better. Among the sixty-eight *charter* schools in the Bronx, seven have garnered the Reward School recognition for high scores accompanied by a strong narrowing of the gap between advantaged and disadvantaged students. All the students in these charters come from the same general pool of students within this low-income area of the South Bronx. The schools are highly varied in their methods, but in the following descriptions you will notice that they all share a common element.

The Bronx Charter School for Better Learning follows the theories of Caleb Gattegno (1911–1988), an educational theorist whose focus was on mathematics instruction and pedagogical method. He held that teaching materials should be carefully arranged and classroom topics should be the same for all children. Although the emphasis is on the creation of engaging teaching materials, the substance is a sequence of knowledge-based, teacher-decided topics common to all students. It's an interesting example of the way that a school with a definite emphasis—in this case, transforming its students into math whizzes—brings with it superior mastery of the other curricular topics. That's also the case in the next example.

The South Bronx Classical Charter School, instead of focusing on mathematics and method, focuses on learning Latin and the ancient Greek and Roman literary classics. The school *also* teaches a full curriculum that is based on a shared-knowledge sequence like the Lyles-Crouch school in Alexandria. So besides studying Latin and the classics, its young pupils are also studying a specific shared-knowledge curriculum that includes a full range of subjects.

The founder of the school, Mr. Lester Long, wrote me this:

I'm happy to report that we have won "Reward School" status for the past 4 years, and in 2014 won the National Blue Ribbon Award. So much of that success is due to building standards-based scopes and sequences [i.e., specific topics], cohesive and interrelated unit plans [i.e., specific subject-matter details for each class], and detailed and flexible lesson plans, all in an organized format for all subjects and grades.

"Commonality" and "coherence of content" is absolutely critical to any school's success. I can absolutely say that our sequences fit that principle, and certainly the Icahn Core Knowledge schools have a record of incredible results (going on 15 years!). I really like your phrase "specificity is the parent of commonality and coherence." I see knowledge as building on itself, and that we learn through analogy (that is, what we already know). For example, small children saying "broccoli is little trees." Without strict specificity the gaps between each step grow too large, and those analogies and metaphors and that coherence gets weaker. And of course, without such connection, we never learn how to compare and contrast.

The third Reward School in the Bronx is the Success Academy Bronx 2. Because of their amazingly high test scores, the Success Academies have been the subject of much press notice and criticism for their supposedly lockstep, "militaristic" approach. But they are clearly doing some key things right, as one discovers from Robert Pondiscio's brilliant 2019 book, *How the Other Half Learns*. Pondiscio shows that the Success schools not only follow a specific sequence of shared topics, they also teach students how to pay close attention to those topics. The topics themselves are based on principles similar to those in the Core Knowledge Sequence. The Success Academy's Elementary School Curriculum describes "core knowledge" in this way:

> We believe that students need a base of knowledge, often referred to by scholars and education experts as "core knowledge," to learn and explore topics that are important to understanding the world around us. For example, if you do not know anything about the history of kings and queens in Europe—which our scholars explore in first grade—it is impossible to understand the American Revolution and why our government is structured the way it is. An increasing number of kids today have extreme deficits in core knowledge, which impede reading comprehension and their acquisition of further knowledge. We address this challenge primarily through reading, but also through quick hits of background knowledge imparted in our Core Knowledge units.

There are seven Icahn Core Knowledge charter schools in the South Bronx, all supervised by Jeffrey Litt. Many years ago,

Jeff became persuaded that the chief difference between an advantaged and a disadvantaged student is background knowledge. He insisted that this missing knowledge could be conveyed in various ways, from a highly disciplined to a gently enticing mode of pedagogy. He favors a gentle approach—quite different from the enforced discipline approach.

In the key area of verbal competence, the students of Jeff's seven core knowledge schools reach proficiency at 30 points higher than the schools in the surrounding district with the same population mix. That's a tremendous, future-determining outcome for those children. Three of the seven schools have won the rare Blue Ribbon award from the US Department of Education for greatly narrowing the gap between advantaged and disadvantaged students. More are destined to do so.

Here's Jeff on his success in bringing his students' parents into the picture through the explicitness and commonality of his curriculum:

E. D. HIRSCH: All the parents know what your curriculum is. At least more or less. Right?

JEFF LITT: Every parent knows. The first week of every month, every parent gets the monthly syllabus for their child, grade by grade. It's also listed online on our website, and on the bulletin boards in the schools. A parent in the city schools, when a child comes home, says "How was your day? Okay, what'd you learn?" The child says "Uh." In our schools, the parent knows specifically what to ask the child. "What did you learn about the solar system today? What did you learn about the Bill of Rights today? What did you learn about X?" We know it's critical for the parent to play a significant role. In other schools, parents don't know what role to play. I don't want parents selling cookies and all that nonsense. I want them to know what their child is being taught, what their child is responsible for learning, and having them demonstrate their knowledge. Every month, the first week.

A few months later, Litt emailed me with excitement to say that the Icahn debate teams won the American Debate League Middle School City Championships in two of the three divisions. Consider what these kids from the South Bronx have accomplished in scoring higher in debate than *any* of their middle school competitors from New York City, New Jersey, and Long Island (in New York, this is called "citywide"), many from highly affluent school districts that always score well.

Effective debate technique depends on accurately gauging the knowledge and values of an audience of strangers, and being able to communicate effectively, sentence by sentence, paragraph by paragraph, in standard American English. Debate requires mastery of shared knowledge of the American public sphere—what your audience knows and does not know, what might be their viewpoints. You won't persuade anybody to your view in debate if you cannot communicate well. And if you do win prizes for debate, you undoubtedly will be able to write well, read well, and learn well.

Like Sheila Durant over at PS 69, Jeff Litt encourages independence and helps students actively *internalize* the common knowledge and ethical laws that make good citizens. This independent-mindedness not only makes for good debaters, it also makes able self-starters at the high school level. *Every* graduating eighth grader in every one of Litt's seven Core Knowledge schools in the South Bronx gained entrance to a top selective high school in New York City! That's even more impressive than winning the citywide debate contests. The selective high schools have apparently learned that eighth graders from Jeff Litt's schools will flourish in the later grades. They are not only knowledgeable; they are mature in their ethics and self-discipline.

"Nobody Leaves"

If the general public doesn't know about Superintendent Jeff Litt, an American hero, plenty of people in the South Bronx know about his seven schools. Out of the nearly 25,000 families who apply for his school's lotteries, typically only the 130 kindergarten spaces are open, because nobody leaves, and Jeff refuses to create big classes. These 130 fortunate students are random winners by the luck of the draw.

There is also almost no student turnover. I called assistant superintendent Dan Garcia to ask about it: "If no student leaves the schools, what happens when a parent gets a job outside the Bronx?"

"Then the parent still sends the child back to the school," he said.

"You mean even if the parent gets a job in some rich district with high-rated schools, they *bus* their child back to the South Bronx? For instance, a parent gets a job in Westchester County and sends his child to school back in the Bronx?"

"That's right. It's happened more than once—and Westchester has to pay our schools. It's the law."

Westchester has the highest median family income in New

York State; the Bronx has the lowest, and the South Bronx has the lowest in the Bronx. I did not ask Mr. Garcia *how* the youngsters got transported every morning from Westchester County, but it's an image that I cannot erase from my mind. Here are seven schools in the South Bronx that are so attractive to parents and children alike that, even when a family moves to a highly rated money-no-object school system, they will not leave their beloved school even though it operates on exactly the same per-pupil budget as the other public schools in the Bronx. The parents are attached to the school, and so are the children. And when they graduate from eighth grade, they all attend top high schools. How is it possible that there has been so little coverage of this Bronx miracle?

Consider the wider implications of these consistent successes. If you lived in the Bronx, and one of Jeff's schools was your regular neighborhood public school, then *your* child would love school and not wish to leave. *Your* child would be so well schooled that he or she could attend a top high school. Imagine such public schools all over the nation; the fortunes of the United States, both economically and socially would soar. Its unity and competence would rise.

So, what is Jeff's secret? There are two characteristics that any American elementary school *could* duplicate. The first is an explicit, planned-out curriculum with the topics clearly defined for all; a curriculum that engages not just the children but also the teachers and the parents. (There's nothing magical involved.) Any similarly specific sequence of topics would work equally well. To see what Jeff's curriculum is, you can download it for free from the Core Knowledge Foundation. (It's too massive to reproduce here.)

The second characteristic of Jeff's schools is a low-pressure atmosphere that does *not* insist on every child reaching the desired goal right away. This aspect reflects Jeff's special humaneness, and it is the origin of the school's motto: "Every child is gifted; some just take longer to unwrap." Indirect social pressure no doubt plays a big role in motivating the child. But the gentle, noninsistent pressure from within that each child feels as a member of the group is equally significant.

A third key element of the schools' culture is that no class is permitted to exceed eighteen students. That restriction was written into Jeff's original charter almost twenty years ago. Small classes suggest the communitarian character of Jeff's vision. That plus rich subject matter leaves no child behind, and keeps no child feeling herself to be a too-slow outsider. Everyone loves the schools—teachers, parents, kids. Nobody leaves.

And if nobody leaves (even if it requires a long commute), that means the class itself becomes not just a speech community but, more broadly, a social community. It's no wonder that 25,000 families apply every year. If such schooling can succeed in the Bronx, it can succeed pretty much anywhere. With seven schools, random assignment of students, and, as of this writing, an eighteen-year track record of success with students with all sorts of disadvantages, the Icahn Core Knowledge schools tell a story that's been too long ignored.

Jeff Litt is a visionary. He deserves a great deal of respect for what he has consistently accomplished over nearly two decades. But his success is not unique. The key difference between *all seven* of the Reward Schools in the South Bronx, and the contrasting results from the hundreds of less successful schools there and across the country, is chiefly the focus on specific topics shared by all students and an imperative to teach actual content to each grade consistently year to year so that knowledge builds on knowledge and an effective speech community is formed.

The point of view that dominates elementary education today is individualistic. But life in adult society is communal. The advent of civilization and the division of labor require cooperation among people. Shared language—social communication—has become the key to a society's progress and competence. And we now know with certainty that the basis of effective social communication is shared knowledge starting in the first years of schooling. That doesn't mean *everyone* ends up knowing exactly the same things. Of course not; there is always a need for idiosyncrasy and quirkiness. But democracy and equality demand a rich public sphere where people are able to communicate effectively with one another.

Let's now get to the root of how, when, and where things went wrong.

CHAPTER 4

The Problem Starts at Our Teacher-Training Institutes

It's not just ignorance. There's active resistance [in our education schools] to the science, too. I interviewed a professor of literacy . . . who told me she was "philosophically opposed" to phonics instruction. One of her colleagues told me she didn't agree with the findings of reading scientists because "it's their science."

—Emily Hanford, "Why Are We Still Teaching Reading the Wrong Way?," *New York Times*, October 2018

Like some zombie that keeps returning from its grave, pure discovery continues to have its advocates. However, anyone who takes an evidence-based approach to educational practice must ask the same question: Where is the evidence that it works?

—Richard E. Mayer, "Should There Be a Three-Strikes Rule against Pure Discovery Learning?," *American Psychologist* (January 2004)

The education our teachers receive today is determined more by ideology and personal predilection than the needs of our children.

—Arthur Levine, former president of Teachers College, Columbia University, *Educating School Teachers* (2006)

A Wrong Theory

We Americans have the means and the national energy to equal the scholastic performance of any nation. Our educational failures must signal that our dominant educational ideas are off kilter. Anyone who compares the ideas that dominate our teacher-training schools with the insights of current cognitive science must recognize their shortcomings. Yet we persist in the wrong direction, because the "nature knows best" point of view is at bottom a quasireligious conviction.

The religious faith in the rightness of nature started appearing in our schooling with the help of William Heard Kilpatrick, John Dewey's colleague at Teachers College. His hugely influential 1918 paper "The Project Method" depicted ordinary schoolchildren as "dawdling" and prone to letting their minds wander. The reason: our schooling was artificial and unappealing to the child, whereas if we gave the child a purposeful project like putting out a school newspaper, she would be filled with "purpose," and would "grow" both socially and intellectually. Filled with purpose, the child would actively learn, not passively dawdle. To quote Kilpatrick:

> The contention of this paper is that wholehearted purposeful activity in a social situation as the typical unit of school procedure is the best guarantee of the utilization of the child's native capacities now too frequently wasted.

So artificial methods of coercion will not work as well as guiding the child's "native capacities."

Over a relatively short time, Kilpatrick's quasireligious "nature knows best" principle of romanticism came to dominate

US educational thought. Quasireligious adherence explains why "whole language" instruction is conceived to be better than explicit phonics, and why natural "discovery learning" is conceived to be better than explicit lectures from a "sage on the stage." (To get the flavor of this intense faith, I suggest that readers, if they have a spare moment, take a look on YouTube at "Progressive Education in the 1940s" [actually shot in 1936]— as an old "March of Time" movie short. There one can catch shots of both William Heard Kilpatrick and John Dewey pronouncing stirring sentiments.)

But even if nature does know best, there's no cogent evidence that nature wants us to do what Kilpatrick and Dewey and our education schools say it wants us to do. Take, for example, the simple but desperately important question of how to teach children to read. In an opinion piece in the *New York Times*, Emily Hanford asks: What's the most effective way to teach children how to decode the visible marks on the printed page into the sounds and words of speech? It's an empirical question, and we have a definitive empirical answer: the fastest, most reliable way of enabling all children to decode print accurately is to teach letter-sound correspondences explicitly and systematically.

According to our schools of education, that "deadly, artificial" mode of instruction must be wrong and deadening because it is not a natural approach. Much better to let the child work out the letter-sound system by a "holistic, immersive" way that mixes phonics "naturally and pleasurably" into a child's exposure to books. This approach became known as "whole language." Insufficiently vetted articles supporting these natural methods were published in educational journals and offered to young future teachers as scientifically valid confirmations giving educators the conviction to say: "They have their science; we have ours."

Because of our educational romanticism, many of our young students *still* struggle to decode print—a moral and an educational scandal! Without that basic decoding ability, the "pleasure" of reading means nothing. Soon, regardless of how much fun they're supposed to be having reading independently about dinosaurs or baseball or ballerinas, reading becomes an exercise in frustration for children who never mastered phonics and can't progress appropriately.

I begin with this example because it offers an insight into the thought world of our teacher-training institutions. In recent decades they have been more like theological seminaries than professional training institutes such as nursing or medical schools. In a nursing school, no professor says: "A nearby medical school has *its* science and we have *ours*." But doctrines in many schools of education *are* at odds with those of other university departments—and especially with those of cognitive psychology. The ed school resistance to anything "unnatural" expresses itself as a resistance to anything that is systematic or arduous. The implicit reasoning goes as follows: That's *not* the way nature works in building the child's body; surely, it's *not* how nature works in building the child's mind.

But paradoxically, nature agrees with the advocates of the artificial. That's because the unseen, instinctive, unconscious workings of nature that guide a child's bodily growth are *not* at work in—and refrain from interfering in—many domains of what a young human being must learn in a tribe or nation.

Science and Philosophy Say Human Instincts Are Unreliable Guides

Spiders, at birth, can immediately begin weaving intricate webs—though no one ever taught them how to do so or even showed them an example. This is instinct. They can catch their food on their own from the start.

Human babies? No. If you leave an infant on its own, useful survival instincts do not kick in. The baby doesn't know how to find food or shelter, how to hunt or defend against predators. Infants can barely move—their best defense is to cry loudly for an adult's help. Nearly everything they do must be taught or modeled by adults.

For humans, nature abandoned instinct and pleasure as the dominant guide because (through evolution) it found that humans survived better when their big, rational, clever brains enabled them to create powerful social arrangements that guaranteed plenty of food and drink, destroyed enemies, and created laws and social norms. *Homo sapiens* evolved. One of our inventions was the writing down of oral speech in visible form. It is a thoroughly cultural, not natural, phenomenon, and it's no surprise that mastery of reading should require a pragmatic, noninstinctual, artificial mode of learning.

Our teachers and our professors of education deeply need to adjust their view of what is natural. Noah Webster's later ally Horace Mann (1796–1859) understood that. In his very first issue of the *Common School Journal*, about the aims of the American public school, he wrote the following:

The human being is less endowed with instincts for his guidance than the lower orders of animated creation.

Consider then his condition when first ushered into life. He is encompassed by a universe of relations, each one of which will prove a blessing or a curse, just according to the position which he may sustain towards it, and yet in regard to all these relations it is to him a universe of darkness.

All his faculties and powers are susceptible of a right direction and control, and, if obedient to them, blessings innumerable and inexhaustible will be lavished upon him. But all his powers and faculties are also liable to a wrong direction and control; and, obedient to them, he becomes a living wound, and the universe of encompassing relations presses upon him only to torture him.

Evolutionary psychologists could not have stated the case more precisely: The latest news from brain science says that Horace Mann was right and the romantic educational theorists who took over American education are wrong. Nature gave us big brains to invent new social arrangements that are supposed sometimes to thwart and control our earlier-evolved instincts.

Not only do our education schools often support a wrong theory about reading, they also support a wrong theory about *how* children should be taught and *what* children should be taught. Both of those fundamental errors stem from the faith that, even at the cultural level, nature is providential, that it is God's agent and therefore benign. This is inconsistent not only with evolutionary psychology but also with the wisdom of philosophers and sages from many cultures and eras.

For most of recorded human history, philosophers, sages, and storytellers have insisted that human instinct is morally unreliable and needs to be guided by laws and rules, not by doing what comes naturally. Romanticism was overconfident about nature. The devil tears at our souls, as much as do the better angels of our nature. So held Shakespeare. There's a scene in *King Lear* in which the murderous bastard Edmund praises nature above the artificial laws and conventions of nations. He sees nature as the triumph of the strongest and most ruthless. That's to Edmund's benefit, and so he soliloquizes: "Thou, nature, art my goddess; to thy law / My services are bound." For Edmund's creator, Shakespeare, nature was an indifferent, sometimes evil goddess. True goodness (Cordelia) is to be found in submitting nature to the control of human moral laws, not to Edmund's lawless individualism.

Evolutionary psychology has come to agree with Shakespeare. In humans, nature is not a socially reliable guide, as the romantics believed. David Sloan Wilson and E. O. Wilson, in a famous article on the complex social workings of evolution, pronounced a now-famous dictum: "Selfishness beats altruism within groups. Altruistic groups beat selfish groups. Everything else is commentary." In other words, it is in the best interest of society and our schools to promote the altruistic thread, and to rein in our selfish selves.

John Dewey's Influence

To get a sense of the guiding ideas behind the teachings of our current education schools, John Dewey is a good place to start. He was by anyone's standards a fine person with admirable social goals, a sharp mind, and an intellectual honesty that makes me think he would readily convert to a post-Dewey, scientifically guided view if he were alive today. Dewey offers a good introduction to the world of the American ed school, where he is held in high regard.

He articulated educational principles that, after a period, dominated America's elementary school education. Here's a characteristic statement of principle from Dewey's early essay "My Pedagogic Creed":

> I believe that this educational process has two sides—one psychological and one sociological; and that neither can be subordinated to the other or neglected without evil results following. Of these two sides, the psychological is the basis. The child's own instincts and powers furnish the material and give the starting point for all education.

Dewey explained that if we conduct such child-centered education properly, following the child's "instincts and powers," we will automatically socialize the child. He said that nature had given humans a social instinct that would ensure a good social result. Since each child has a different nature, to offer *each* child the *same* curriculum would be unnatural. In the first quarter of the twentieth century, this idea led to child-centered education and progressive education. Its chief feature, besides its faith in hands-on projects rather than bookish approaches, was the idea that the school curriculum should be individualized to suit the nature of the individual child.

When child-centered personalization of schooling was first implemented in a few American schools in the early twentieth century, it was attacked as being too content-vague and too individualized. Critics, including many teachers, objected, "How could anyone keep track of what the students were learning or needed to learn if each child was doing special projects and following individual paths?" John Dewey, the accepted intellectual leader of the early movement, conceded the problem. But not to worry: the child's special nature, being conscientiously followed, would rescue the situation and make things right.

Dewey therefore wrote an influential book a decade later, *How We Think* (1910), whose basic argument was that our schools are *really* teaching something beyond mere content—namely, critical thinking skills.

> Our teachers find their tasks made heavier in that they have come to deal with pupils individually and not merely in mass. Unless these steps in advance are to end in distraction, some clue of unity, some principle that makes for simplification, must be found. This book represents the conviction that the needed steadying and centralizing factor is found in adopting as the end of endeavor that attitude of mind, that habit of thought, which we call scientific.

Dewey was right about the structure of the difficulty, but later work in psychology has demolished his proposed solution. As chapter 5 will show in detail, there *is* no reliable general expertise of "scientific thinking" or "critical thinking," despite its being invoked continually in the mission statements of our public schools. Yet without identifying critical thinking as the goal, one cannot easily justify the drawbacks of incoherent helter-skelter school content. Dewey himself said as much.

For Americans to persist now in slogans and goals that

cannot be supported either by psychology or good school results is morally blameworthy. No child can find individual self-fulfillment in a modern society while lacking in social competence, including effective speaking, reading, and writing, all of which are dependent on shared knowledge. Real individualism and independence of thought comes after cognitive and linguistic mastery—not before. Just as any great musician must begin with scales and simple repetition before improvising and creating something great, so must our children first get down the accepted currency of communication before we should expect them to follow their own intellectual paths.

What Is Personalized Education?

Nowadays, the term used for this child-centered approach is "personalization." In practice, that's the main principle of educational romanticism. It's the key doctrine that has vitiated our teacher training. It's also the chief idea that needs to be adjusted in that training.

There are two diverse (often muddled) meanings to the idea of "personalized" education. One version advises teachers to choose individualized *topics* that are congenial to the tastes and predilections of each individual child. That is what John Dewey meant when he said that "the child's own instincts and powers *furnish the material* and give the starting point for all education." In practice, that doctrine has implied offering different content to different children, especially in the key subject of language arts.

It is absolutely the case that good elementary school teaching needs to include personalized instruction. Nonetheless, it has been a fundamental conceptual error to assume that this idea implies personalizing the *topics* of instruction. A much superior version of personalized teaching borrows from the biblical idea of teaching as "accommodation." Just as God accommodated His message in the Bible to the limited capacity of human understanding, so the teacher and the preacher must accommodate their message to the capacity of the flock and the individuals within it. Such accommodation is a key principle of effective teaching too. An excellent teacher is able to offer all children the *same* underlying topics and ideas, but the shared content will be accommodated to each child's level.

In this approach, all the children in the classroom have in common the basic background knowledge they need even as they are encouraged to grasp in their own ways what is being discussed. In early language development, as a whole, individualism is not the friend but the enemy. If we want to impart verbal proficiency, we need to impart shared knowledge through a shared curriculum.

Once the social and linguistic need for commonality in background knowledge is understood, the classroom becomes a little society in which the members understand one another and make progress. But without such commonality, Milton's great line in *Lycidas* applies: "The hungry sheep look up and are not fed."

Constructivism

Sometime around 1960, after the term "progressivism" fell into disrepute, and the general public started making fun of the anti-intellectual consequences of doing projects rather than learning reading and writing and arithmetic (not to mention literature, science, history, and civics), our schools of education adopted the term "constructivism" to continue following the same naturalistic methods introduced by progressivism, but without the drawback of the mockery to which it had been subjected.

"Constructivism" carries respect in cognitive psychology, but as used in education policy is incorrect. Constructivism in mainline psychology proposes that our minds construct what they see, hear, and learn. For example, if we close one eye and look out the window at trees or buildings, our single eye can see only two dimensions. But we have learned to construct what we see with one eye as being three-dimensional, though we are actually seeing just two dimensions. The same is true when we observe a two-dimensional painting or a photo. We construct or interpret three dimensions. When we listen to speech on the radio, we don't just passively receive meaning; we actively construct meaning from the sounds. That view of constructivism is basically the point that Immanuel Kant made in the eighteenth century, when he showed that the mind doesn't just receive but also shapes, or "constructs," what it knows.

The term is used by education professors to keep the project method going. The teaching mantra today is "Don't be a sage on the stage!" Instead, teachers are advised to use techniques like "cooperative learning," which is a way of encouraging students of varied abilities and knowledge to work together teaching one another; "inquiry-based instruction," which encourages students to ask their own questions and think about their own ideas to improve their problem-solving skills; "discovery learning," which is the old project-based activity of progressive education, or "project-based learning," which is the same thing.

Constructivism in its scientifically respectable sense makes no claims about the best ways to conduct schooling, and it carries no special implications for education. It is a general principle that holds for all perception and learning. In its accurate form it says that all forms of schooling are constructivist—even when students listen to lectures from a "sage on the stage." Contrary to what our teachers are being told, in a whole-class session led by a good teacher, the students are actively and successfully constructing meaning from what they hear. And, as teachers testify, when well done, it's the liveliest classroom to be found!

When elementary school children learn multiple different topics without progression or coherence by choosing their own projects, topics, and subject matters, learning can be extremely slow and disorganized. The adoption of progressivism as the official mode of instruction (under a different name) has ensured the educational decline of the United States.

The term "constructivism" is a rhetorical trick, a scientific-sounding term used to preserve the outmoded theories and practices of educational romanticism. It reduces the amount of time the teacher engages with a child and increases the time that the untutored young are tutoring each other—*without a license.*

The Constructivist Curriculum I: "Reading and Writing" and "Literature" Became "Language Arts"

"Language arts" was the new name that constructivist educators gave to studies that had been earlier divided into two subjects: "reading and writing" and "literature." In the early grades these do represent two separate kinds of content. Learning the skills of deciphering and enciphering and correctly spelling written marks is a subject matter in its own right, separate from the various literary topics of poetry and fiction.

But under the new name "language arts" both kinds of text were merged. Decoding and encoding (i.e., phonics), became denatured and mistaught. Children were supposed to learn how to decode and encode speech in the same holistic way they had learned how to listen and talk. "Whole language" carried the naive idea that alphabetic reading and writing (which is a very late human invention) could be assimilated to a child's natural development. These incorrect, sentimental views caused a blossoming of students' inability to read and write.

The heart of child-centered education is still Dewey's old institution, Teachers College, Columbia University. The Teachers College Reading and Writing Project sells classroom libraries between 500 and 750 small, colorful books for each classroom at each grade level, graded by difficulty and on multiple topics that a child might find interesting: *In the Park*, *I Can't Find My Roller Skates*, *Tiny and the Snow Dog*, *Baby Elephant Is Thirsty*. If these attractive texts were used sparingly as take-home recreational practice books, that would be fine. But to use them instead of a coherent knowledge-based curriculum presents a missed opportunity. No one should object to encouraging children to read whatever they want outside school, but it is a huge missed opportunity to make helter-skelter child-chosen content the substance of language arts in the classroom.

For kindergarten, there are 706 books for $4,600, and for first grade, 689 books for $4,200. Schools are expected to buy this whole collection so their children always have lots of options. The teacher is advised to steer the child to a shelf of the proper difficulty level, on whatever topic captures the interest of the individual child. The scheme has not worked very well in raising reading scores, but one would not know that from the Teachers College website, which promotes the classroom library scheme with an imposing bibliography of 154 scientific articles that allegedly support its principles.

The Teachers College project epitomizes many of the most questionable and impractical features of constructivist, child-centered education—the chief one being the idea that the child should be in charge of the lesson topic. Further, it supports the idea that *any* attractive storybook will improve reading facility and add to a child's store of background knowledge. The key strategy of the project is to keep the child interested and reading. That's not entirely wrong, of course. No one would deny that the Teachers College scheme is better than nothing at all. But, as current science has shown, it is not optimal, and especially not for students from disadvantaged circumstances.

The positive effects of constructivist education are said to be "imaginativeness," "creativity," and "happiness." But there is no *persuasive* evidence to show that adults who are products of constructivist education are happier and more fulfilled, or more creative than those who are products of a coherent common curriculum. In fact, if school enthusiasm and high morale are any indication, the opposite is true. Knowledge-based schooling seems to make students eager and happy, for ignorance is no friend to creativity. In sum, the effect of constructivist theory on learning language and literature has been negative, and the prevalence of this method in the United States helps explain the decline in reading scores recorded in *A Nation at Risk*.

The Constructivist Curriculum II: History and Civics Fell by the Wayside

Just as with the case of language arts, the constructivists also decided to rename other aspects of elementary education. The former rubrics for elementary school subject matters—for instance, "American history"—encouraged the teacher to impart the specific knowledge directly rather than through projects whereby the student could construct learning for herself, or through the child's own account of "me, my family, my school, my community." History took on the vaguer title "social studies."

The name change "social studies" brought with it an abandonment of history as a serious subject in elementary school. That abandonment of coherent content became the pattern for the whole of the elementary curriculum, which was now to be natural and "developmentally appropriate." Facts became inconvenient burdens. After all, it is hard not to be a "sage on the stage" if one decides to teach young children something about American history from colonial times to the election of Ulysses S. Grant. Or the "mere fact" that the Civil War occurred between 1861 and 1865.

The effect of constructivism on the learning of history and civics has been equally negative. In neglecting the coherent teaching of history in the early grades, it ushered in a new ignorance of American culture, ideals, and history. Here's a succinct report from the distinguished educational historian Diane Ravitch:

In 1982 I began to research the condition of history instruction in the public schools. The more closely I examined the social studies curriculum, the more my attention was drawn to the curious nature of the early grades, which is virtually content-free. The social studies curriculum for the K–3 grades is organized around the study of the relationships within the home, school, neighborhood, and local community. This curriculum of "me, my family, my school, my community" now dominates the early grades in American public education. It contains no mythology, legends, biographies, hero tales, or great events in the life of this nation or any other.

The idea behind this version of an "appropriate" early curriculum is the "expanding environments" idea, which holds that we have to start not by teaching the history, songs, and stories that help define the culture, but rather that we proceed by engaging the concrete, everyday experiences of the child's natural development.

The results have increased the ignorance of citizens and have been harmful to the political and civic life of the nation. Here's how a 2003 report from the Thomas B. Fordham Institute describes the way in which constructivist "social studies" took over our elementary schools in the 1930s and 1940s:

> Expanding environments is the basic curriculum that most states, textbook companies, and curriculum leaders use to organize elementary (K–6) social studies, and it has dominated elementary school social studies for nearly 75 years. The basic premise is that at each grade level, each year, students are exposed to a slowly widening social

environment that takes up, in turn, self/home (kindergarten), families (1st grade), neighborhoods (2nd), communities (3rd), state (4th), country (5th), and world (6th). While this approach appears to provide an organized curricular sequence, it lacks substantial content, especially in the early elementary grades, and children tend to find its narrow focus deeply boring. In fact, expanding environments actually impedes content knowledge because of its trivial and repetitious sequence. For example, students in grades K–3 are taught about "community helpers" like mail carriers, milkmen, and firefighters. Such lessons are superfluous (what kindergartener does not know about firefighters?) but more damagingly do not even begin to lay the groundwork for later study of history, heroes, struggles, victories, and defeats. Instead, they limit children's instruction to persons and institutions with which children are already familiar.

A Nation at Risk informed us that mastery of language was not being effectively achieved. Ravitch's work explained that our history and ideals were not being taught. Those two fundamental aims in making citizens had been front and center in American schooling from the ratification of the Constitution through the first quarter of the twentieth century. The significant drop in results caused by the constructivist view is astonishing.

Unsurprisingly, the National Assessment of Educational Progress (NAEP) reports that Americans' factual knowledge about their nation's history, its ideals, and the details of its form of government has declined sharply since the 1970s. An alarmed organization called the Civic Mission of the Schools recently listed the results of this change in focus:

- In recent years, civic learning has been increasingly pushed aside. In the elementary grades, civic learning used to be woven through the curriculum. Today, slightly more than a third of teachers report covering civic education–related subjects on a regular basis.

- Two-thirds of students scored below "proficient" on a national civics assessment administered in 2010. Less than half of eighth graders surveyed knew the purpose of the Bill of Rights; only one in ten had age-appropriate knowledge of the system of checks and balances among our branches of government. These results are the same as the results of the two prior national assessments in civics, conducted in 2006 and 1998.

- Scores on the 2010 NAEP were even lower for low-income and minority students, with black students scoring, on average, 24 to 30 points lower than their white counterparts. This persistent civic achievement gap undermines the equality of all citizens.

To reverse this trend, an early move of any civic-minded reformer of our education should be to rename the subject "history and civics" as before, and outline the grade-by-grade knowledge of history and civics to be learned.

Let's now examine the effects of educational romanticism on classroom teaching.

Constructivism Bites the Intellectual Dust: The Wider Implications of the Whole-Language Fiasco

Emily Hanford's wonderfully written piece on the subject of language instruction, entitled "Why Are We Still Teaching Reading the Wrong Way?," names numerous first-rate experimental studies showing the superiority of an "instructivist" approach to teaching phonics. She describes the resistance of US education professors to promulgate current research, with the tragic result being that a lot of American children still cannot read fluently.

Nothing is more important in modern education than teaching children how to decode print quickly and accurately. Why would our ed schools still sponsor a failed approach? The answer is to be found in a remark by Arthur Levine, the distinguished past president of Teachers College, Columbia University. "The education our teachers receive today is determined more by ideology and personal predilection than the needs of our children."

Here's an example: In 2006, the distinguished cognitive psychologist Paul A. Kirschner and two of his colleagues wrote a decisive article: "Why Minimal Guidance During Instruction Does Not Work: An Analysis of the Failure of Constructivist, Discovery, Problem-Based, Experiential, and Inquiry-Based Teaching." It's useful reading for any scholar or concerned parent who might want to dig deeper. The best researchers in the constructivist tradition *tried* to answer Kirschner and his colleagues. A 2007 article in response said that not all discovery methods were ineffective, since some of them used "scaffolding." That is to say, students are offered the background knowledge they need up to a point and *then* are to figure things out for themselves without benefit of guidance. In fact, this is a good description of ordinary "instructivist" teaching, except that if the students don't figure out the right inference in a reasonable amount of time, it gets explained to them, and the class moves on.

Although most quality schools of education have finally conceded that the "whole language" approach must be abandoned and the explicit teaching of phonics adopted, they need to take the next step. Instead of seeing the failure to teach phonics as a small failure off in the corner, it must be seen as a typical example of the general failure of constructivism as a teaching and learning principle.

The whole-language fiasco happens to be the most decisively studied comparison of implicit versus explicit pedagogy. It contravenes educational romanticism, but schools of education haven't instituted a new approach in response. Unfortunately, most teachers have had to come to this conclusion by their own discovery *after* leaving graduate school. And many of them never do, for they have been explicitly indoctrinated in a false religion, and they hold on to it religiously.

Accurate educational theories have tremendous practical importance for our nation. The administrators of our universities should start actively integrating their ed schools—and especially their ed students—into productive association with other departments on campus. Administrators should insist that there should cease to be a conflict between accurate research in the sciences and humanities and the ideological, often incorrect doctrines promulgated in our schools of education. One step would be to insist that all prospective teachers must take an educational psychology course. It's an unacceptable intellectual (and practical) disgrace that any incongruence between consensus science and teacher training should persist.

The Effect on Disadvantaged Students

Lisa Delpit, a brilliant African American educator, had critical things to say about constructivist methods in teaching African American students in her book *Other People's Children* (1995). She pointed out that the language of the classroom itself was often meaningless to black students and to other students whose language and shared knowledge was not that of the American print culture that more advantaged American kids absorbed at home. She was particularly critical of methods that we now call constructivist: discovery learning, inquiry learning, and methods that ask children to work things out for themselves. How are they supposed to do that? she asked. They don't know what you are talking about.

She was describing the very troubling problem that got me started in the 1980s in educational research. I was gathering some data among freshmen at the University of Virginia, and I decided to broaden the inquiry to include students at a then mostly black college, the J. Sargeant Reynolds Community College. There I got back a lot of blank sheets. The students hadn't a clue as to the question I was asking. The question itself had taken too much for granted. Experiences like that, plus immersing myself in psycholinguistics and other branches of cognitive psychology, forcefully brought home the role of unheard and unseen knowledge in understanding speech and writing.

To be a disadvantaged child is to lack the modes of speech, the vocabulary, and the shared knowledge of the national print culture. Kids who come from circumstances in which the language of the home is standard educated English possess both language and background knowledge that enables them to move forward in school, even when the teacher asks them to find things out for themselves. The essence of school disadvantage is the lack of requisite prior knowledge to understand, much less perform, a particular task. In the psychological literature, the distinction is drawn between "novices" and "experts."

The only way the construct-it-for-yourself mode of teaching can work for a child is if she has adequate prior background knowledge to deduce the right inferences. Disadvantaged children usually lack the background knowledge to be able to pull out the right inference from discovery-based methods. The discovery method will therefore tend to *increase* the gap between advantaged and disadvantaged children. Possessing less knowledge of the print culture, they will not reliably understand the language of the classroom, and they will be able to construct far fewer new learnings from the small-group projects and learning centers of child-centered instruction.

But those same disadvantaged students, when given explicit whole-class, sage-on-the-stage instruction, *will gain relatively more than advantaged kids will*. Here's why: they have much more to learn. For they have to amass the needed *prior* knowledge as well as the knowledge focused on within the lesson itself. This explains the Grissmer results noted in chapter 3, in which explicit shared-knowledge instruction caused advantaged students to gain half a standard deviation over constructed-learning students, even though *it caused disadvantaged students to gain two-thirds of a standard deviation over their counterparts in the constructivist classroom*. In short, anybody who favors the principle of equality should favor a definite shared-knowledge curriculum taught by the most effective means, which is almost always through compelling, explicit modes of instruction. This is particularly true in elementary school, when everyone is a novice, and it's emphatically so for disadvantaged students.

Here's the way the distinguished cognitive scientists Richard E. Clark, Paul A. Kirschner, and John Sweller sum up the inutility and harm of constructivist methods in the early grades.

After a half century of advocacy associated with instruction using minimal guidance instruction, it appears that there is no body of sound research that supports using the technique with anyone other than the most expert students. Evidence from controlled, experimental (a.k.a. "gold standard") studies almost uniformly supports full and explicit instructional guidance rather than partial or minimal guidance for novice to intermediate learners. . . . Teachers should provide their students with clear, explicit instruction rather than merely assisting students in attempting to discover knowledge themselves.

PART II

Science Debunks Child-Centered Education

CHAPTER 5

Culture, Not Nature, Knows Best—Says Nature

Let us then suppose the mind to be, as we say, white paper, void of all characters without any ideas. How comes it to be furnished? Whence comes it by that vast store which the busy and boundless fancy of man has painted on it with an almost endless variety? Whence has it all the materials of reason and knowledge? To this I answer in one word, from EXPERIENCE.

—John Locke, *Essay Concerning Human Understanding* (1690)

I t's not the fault of our teachers that our students are performing poorly in international comparisons, or that our disadvantaged students lag ever further behind as they proceed through the grades. Instead, the main fault lies with the seductive "child centered" ideas drilled into our teachers' minds, and into the minds of school administrators and state officials— ideas based on the concept that education is partly a matter of drawing out the child's inborn nature.

There *Is* No Inborn Blueprint for a Child's Mental "Development"

"Development" is a term one hears frequently in early education. Its most significant advocate in the twentieth century was Jean Piaget. In 1936 he published his theory of education, which held that there were four distinct stages of a child's development, each corresponding with the child's biological maturation:

- Sensorimotor (birth to age two; primarily concerned with learning object permanence)
- Preoperational (two to seven years; learning to think symbolically)
- Concrete operational (seven to eleven years; thinking more logically and able to work things out mentally without having to see solutions physically)
- Formal operational (eleven years and up; gaining the ability to think abstractly and test hypotheses)

He listed many specific skills to go along with each of these four stages. I'd point you to them, except that they're incorrect. Still, in the second half of the twentieth century, having nothing better to go on, most professionals have accepted Piaget's work as fact, and his theory has become the prevailing American assumption about how children learn. These developmental stages were especially attractive to our experts because they fit in well with the "nature knows best" conception.

Anything that seemed hard and artificial for the young child (explicit phonics, for instance) was deemed wrong, harmful, and "developmentally inappropriate." That phrase, "developmentally appropriate practice," pronounced authoritatively, has been a dangerous hindrance to American excellence in early education. It advised withholding challenging material from young children that they might eagerly learn if they had the preparatory knowledge to do so. The authority of Piaget has sustained this bullying and misguided phrase.

Teachers and parents should therefore be wary of "developmentally appropriate practice." It can stand in the way of progress for your child. Of course, "readiness to learn" is definitely a sound idea. But what a child is ready to learn largely depends on what she has *already* learned. The chief thing to keep reminding yourself of is that the child's mental development does not inherently follow the child's physical development. The body has a defined blueprint. The mind does not. The little French children in the preschool schoolyard look like the children over here, except that they're all speaking French! Their mental "development" in their very different culture clearly was different. Education is chiefly "instructivism" from the surrounding culture more than "constructivism" from within the soul of the child.

Science tells us several other key things about learning that we need to make our schools aware of, and which on the whole run counter to their thinking. The first overarching one is that we need to return to the Enlightenment idea that the child's mind is chiefly a blank slate. Evolution has worked it out so that instead of following instinct like the fruit fly, we humans must develop our own rules of conduct, as dictated by the big social group we find ourselves in, so that our big, smart brains will, through group cooperation, defeat—and if necessary kill off—other species or other human tribes that pose a danger.

Evolution has enabled this cooperation through the development of an enlarged energy-expensive part of the brain that occupies 80 percent of its current total mass: the neocortex. It is so large that birth is painful and dangerous, but its size is worth it statistically, because it fosters survival. Evolution also has made our brains *qualitatively* different from those of our ancestors, with the help of a new *kind* of brain cell, not found in other species. It's called the "rosehip" neuron, and it is able to control events in other distant neurons. In other words, it's not just the enlarged *mass* of the cortex that makes our learning and thinking more effective than that of other species, it's also the evolution of more competent cells within the brain itself.

How Do We Know That There Is No Innate Blueprint?

A key subject of child development is not simply the maturation of the individual child and her brain, but also the development of the *Homo sapiens* brain itself over hundreds of thousands of generations. Knowing how the human brain evolved (about which we are learning more and more) lends insight into its character and function. Here's the most important takeaway to date as it relates to education:

The brain's latest-evolved part—the neocortex, the big part that lies over other parts that evolved earlier and controls them—is largely a blank slate, just as John Locke argued. Locke's basis for saying so was his observation of the large variations in human cultures and in human tastes and interests. Given the same organic structure, why were humans so variable in their interests, tastes, and cultures? One big source, Locke argued, could be the variability of their experiences, including their formal educations. So, experience must play a decisive role. Moreover, there was a Latin saying from ancient times that Locke knew well: *nihil in intellectu nisi prius in sensu*—"Nothing in the mind unless first in the senses." That is largely true of the neocortex.

The current focus of brain science is on this latest-evolved brain part, because it's the general of the cognitive army, recently promoted by evolution to foster human survival and the flourishing of the species. It's responsible for a lot of higher-order brain functions, including issuing motor commands, interpreting sensory perceptions, thinking abstractly, solving problems, remembering the spatial relations of objects, and, above all, communicating via language. In it resides memory for words and meaning. Damage to the neocortex destroys a person's language ability. It's the center for most of the characteristics that distinguish us from other creatures.

One way to think of the neocortex is as the chief residence for culture, the creator of the tribes and societies that enable humans to prevail in conflict by coordinating their actions in space and over time in ways that no single creature could accomplish alone. Apes form groups, but small ones. Only large groups can create special occupations and elaborate social organizations to defeat large, dangerous creatures, and, alas, other human tribes. The chief function of human education is the initiation of the boy or girl into the tribe—and thence, over the history of civilization, into the city and the nation. Education is not, in humans, chiefly for the benefit of the individual, but for the group. At the *individual* level of animal life, all the brain functions needed for survival can be accomplished with a much smaller brain. The solitary lifestyle does not need to curb, control, and channel its selfish orientation. It does not need language. The size of the neocortex grew big because of the complex needs associated with making a workable society that can become an overwhelming foe when acting in unison. The larger neocortex encouraged the evolutionary ability to make a society possible, and to put an agency of control over theft, lust, envy—all those vices repudiated in the Ten Commandments. The neocortex became the maker of the means of communication and of rules of conduct that enable a society to thrive. The neocortex is chiefly where civilization resides.

So, What's New (Neo) about the Neocortex?

Our ability to connect a lot of diverse and disparate brain synapses gives us not just language but also other capacities unique among living things. Researchers in brain science use the term "plasticity" instead of the old phrase "blank slate." It's a different metaphor that means the same thing. Instead of being a blank slate on which things can be written, the implicit metaphor is of a piece of clay that can be molded. The nerve cells of the brain can be taught new things. Two other metaphors used in this research are "rewiring" and "microcircuit," taken from electronics. They're not too far-fetched, since the nervous impulses themselves are electric. All three metaphors are useful in different contexts.

The debate over early education and the young brain is easily settled by the latest research on the neocortex. In 2005, Nir Kalisman, a brain researcher, published an article entitled "The Neocortical Microcircuit as a *Tabula Rasa*" ("blank slate"). As Professor Kalisman confirmed in an email to me,

"The biological circuitry in the cortex is so flexible as to allow any form of knowledge and behavior to be taught to it." Hundreds of research studies since have supported the Kalisman findings, including a more recent one in Hungary in which tests on mature, living ("*in vivo*") neocortical tissues were conducted. This cannot be done ethically under normal circumstances, but ethical issues do not arise if the tissue comes from a necessary operation that removes some brain tissue.

The research showed that the human brain has become more flexible and more able to learn quickly because of the structure and functions of uniquely human cortex cells, which can conduct unique operations at the cellular level. We evolved not only bigger brains, but also ones with smarter, more flexible cells that enable symbolic functions and language, central to our culture-making abilities. Let's agree, then, that the neocortex does not arrive in the world with any significant "text" written on it—that it is basically a blank state, as Locke predicted. What are some of the implications for educational policy and for the way we decide what and how to teach our children?

But first a caveat: Evolutionary psychology, anthropology, and brain studies have reached a kind of truce in which scientists agree that there are indeed universal, built-in precultural universals across human societies (hence there is a human nature), but that human nature is highly malleable in detail through social enforcement and education. We all have inherited tendencies both as a species and as the child of particular parents, but the recent work I have cited also argues that the human brain is a big blank slate, open to a social education that has the power to override and control our often-conflicting impulses.

The Blank Slate and the American Dream

The bright significance of these recent studies of cortical plasticity is that individual humans and human societies can make and remake themselves. We can make a new nation, and out of immigrants we can make new citizens. Our inborn tendencies are emphatically present, but that same neocortex, well socialized, guides and controls impulses and prescribes ethical action for the sake of the group. That is a chief function of the neocortex and its ally, education: it forms new circuits and synapses that make us moral and competent, and induces our loyalties to the wider group as well as to our immediate family and neighbors. Self-fulfillment is, equally, an achievable goal within that social architecture.

We are lucky that America was created by Enlightenment thought, with its preromantic, clear-eyed recognition of the unsavory impulses beneath our social ideals. Our Constitution was formed with a keen eye to human contradictions and foibles. Its chief author, James Madison, said this:

> As there is a degree of depravity in mankind which requires a certain degree of circumspection and distrust: So there are other qualities in human nature, which justify a certain portion of esteem and confidence. Republican government presupposes the existence of these [more estimable] qualities in a higher degree than any other form.

Those better angels exist only partly in our evolved emotional sympathies. They reside chiefly in our long-term memories, placed there by education. Lucky for us, our founders had read John Locke, not just his theoretical wirings on nation making, but also his blank slate theory. The Constitution and the other qualities justifying Madison's "esteem" have so far prevailed.

The American idea gradually evolved into the idea of deliberate self-transformation. An individual can become a new person, an American. America was to embrace everyone who wanted to belong, and, for the more radical thinkers in the North, like Herman Melville, this new person could be of any race or former nationality. That's adhering to the blank-slate principle on a big scale, and it has profound relevance to our current internal conflicts over race and ethnicity.

That issue is a chief reason neocortical research is currently so important. It shows that ethnicity is not inherent but learned. It can be altered. It can be accompanied by a second ethnicity with equal authenticity. By education it can be unmade and made.

The Blank Slate and the Ambiguities of "Ethnicity"

The great enemy to the American vision is essentialism, which says that your ethnicity or race is who you are in your unchangeable essence. Ethnicity is possibly the most fraught political-social issue of our time, not just in the United States but around the world. Tribalism is a human universal. A key question of human history is whether the Enlightenment hope for broad, universalistic tribalism (*Alle Menschen werden brueder*; *Liberté, Egalité, Fraternité*) is achievable through education.

When the United States was founded in 1776, the chief conflict in Europe was between Catholics and Protestants. The Wars of the Reformation killed hundreds of thousands. Our founders were wary. They were well aware that the potential for such conflict was ever present in human nature. So they excluded the possibility of a national religion and sought to create a government that would accommodate every person of every religion, race, and ethnicity. The Declaration of Independence said that governments were instituted to allow us to live safely and in peace. There was to be no establishment of religion or of any other danger to our peace and our free pursuit of happiness. We Americans, they said, aren't trapped by our parents, grandparents, or anybody else.

The fundamental value to society of the blank slate insight is that it defeats the impulse to narrowly essentialize ethnicity. The current intense moralizing about multiculturalism, diversity, identity, race, and intersectionality is of course pointing in the correct ethical direction. But we must beware of the thin ice. The idea that identity and ethnicity are inborn and indelible from birth is a false view that leads to group hostility. The essentializing of ethnicity (as something permanent and unchanging) has helped confuse our current fractured discourse on diversity and multiculturalism. Diversity is not inconsistent with national unity, and it is not morally superior to unity. In the United States, our sense of unity based on our equality is an ethical imperative. In that context, diversity is an aesthetic category, not an ethical one. Diversity gets a moral dimension only when we say we should honor every human culture and racial type—not merely for the sake of diversity as such, but in accord with the moral principle of equality.

Our Enlightenment-era founders were quite profound in conceiving that we could fashion ourselves into a new, broader ethnicity based on sound ethical and political principles. That leaves the way open to individuals adopting more than one cultural identity simultaneously, just as they can readily learn more than one language. It puts new light on the centuries-long American debate over whether a nation should properly be, culturally speaking, a melting pot or a salad bowl.

The new brain studies say: "Hold on! That's not an either-or proposition." An individual does not need to choose one or the other, and neither does a nation. The either-or proposition is essentialist; it assumes that you must give up one identity if you adopt another. This is wrong. All of us have multiple social identities, and none of them is the essential "me." And in a modern nation, one of those identities—the chief one—needs to be one that is shared with other citizens, all of whom are equally fellow Americans with the same basic identity, rights, and privileges as our own.

A nation, to become a *people*, needs to insist on creating a public sphere with shared knowledge that unifies its population and enables its members to work together, communicate effectively with one another, and feel loyalty to one another. At a minimum, its people need to be bicultural—to feel at home locally and nationally. Unity in diversity has been an American success story. Federalism—the political encouragement of diversity within a national unity—has been a virtue that we were forced into by the accidents of our founding. We were compelled to form a union out of semiautonomous states, rather than forming a single monolithic state. This historical accident has so far kept us stable in what Arthur M. Schlesinger Jr. calls the "vital center."

Our founders believed that the common school had a key role to play in moving toward the goal of achieving unity in the federal system. It was to be the instrument that binds us together in civic duty toward the good of the whole, fostering the "general welfare."

The Nature of Skills

By the time the US National Academy of Sciences publishes a book, its contents have been approved by enough special committees to assure us that it represents a firm scientific consensus. In 2000, the Academy released a book called *How People Learn: Brain, Mind, Experience, School.* Its focus was on the individual mind of the student. The key concept was the domain specificity of all human skills, and the nonexistence of the various general skills like critical thinking that our schools claim to teach today.

Almost two decades later, in 2018, the academy released a second volume: *How People Learn II: Learners, Contexts, and Cultures.* Reflecting the latest research, it offered some significant additions. The focus in this latest version is no longer the individual mind alone, but the individual mind as it is conditioned and fostered by the shared knowledge, language, and values of a society. It reports a striking consensus that human learning does *not* reliably follow the traditional Piagetian stages. That's because school learning is chiefly a social process.

These findings, which I am going to summarize, have passed muster over two volumes issued by the National Academy of Sciences, an organization whose membership keeps in touch with science worldwide. Its members are the most esteemed scientists in the nation. The fact that *these* findings are inconsistent with what is often being taught in most American colleges of education is one reason the wider public needs to know what this current science is saying. We need to exert pressure on our schools and our teacher-training institutions to attend to current science, which is the closest thing we have to the reality principle. All of us have an interest in getting our schools of education up to date. The now rapidly growing scientific consensus is that the parts of the mind devoted to language mastery, general competence, and higher-order thinking are *not* governed by natural development or general processing skills but by the explicit and coherent teaching of lots of factual knowledge—by those "mere facts" that are often scorned by those who instruct our teachers.

The Need for Facts I: Skills Are Domain Specific

The most important *educational* finding from recent science can be found in volume 1 of *How People Learn*. It's far from new, but it's still not widely known outside cognitive science. It's called the "domain specificity of human skills." What this means is that being good at tennis does not make you good at golf or soccer. You may be a talented person with great hand-eye coordination—and indeed, there *are* native general abilities that can be nurtured in different ways—but being a first-class swimmer will not make a person good at hockey.

"Critical thinking," like all skills, is drenched in specific knowledge about specific subject matter. Yet it's hard to run across an American school mission statement that doesn't posit "critical thinking" as a general skill—and now included are the "twenty-first-century skills" of "collaboration, communication, critical thinking, and creativity." Even though these don't exist as teachable skills, they still represent the reliable fallback position in defending the absence of specific shared content in our public schools:

New York City: "Instruction is customized, inclusive, motivating, and aligned to the [content-unspecific] Common Core. High standards are set in every classroom. Students are actively engaged in ambitious intellectual activity and developing critical thinking skills."

Los Angeles: "Ensure students reach proficiency in content knowledge and build their critical thinking, collaboration, creativity, and digital skills to achieve the district's graduate profile so all students are efficacious, influential, worldly-wise and adaptable, ready to activate their goals in the 21st Century."

Chicago: "Our goal at Chicago Public Schools is to develop resilient, critical thinkers with the knowledge and skills necessary to meet the demands of a technology-driven world. We must give our students the foundation to solve problems and tackle complex issues that face current and future generations."

One top researcher, Anders Ericsson, is quite blunt on the nonexistence of these skills:

A crucial fact about expert performance in general: there is no such thing as developing a general skill. You don't train your memory; you train your memory for strings of digits or for collections of words or for people's faces. You don't train to become an athlete; you train to become a gymnast or a sprinter or a marathoner or a swimmer or a basketball player.

We are not talking about differences in abilities. We know that some people *are* more generally competent than others. The scientific literature on IQ is clear on that issue, showing that at least 50 percent of one's IQ level is determined by heredity. But while there are general inborn *mechanisms* in the brain, and while some brains are natively smarter than others, those brains can't be marshaled effectively and skillfully without a knowledge base that is fact dependent. That's the key reason a good education can make you smarter.

The Need for Facts II: General Reading Comprehension Skills Don't Exist Either

Nowhere is the domain specificity of knowledge more urgent than in language comprehension itself. Once a child has mastered phonics, the rest of reading is no longer about decoding individual words, but about decoding the *meanings* of sentences and paragraphs. From that point forward, reading comprehension skills have a lot to do with the child's background knowledge.

The pioneers in getting that point across were the cognitive scientists Walter Kintsch and Teun A. van Dijk, who explained why competence in reading comprehension and writing are not general skills:

One of the major contributions of psychology is the recognition that much of the information needed to understand a text is not provided by the information expressed
in the text itself but must be drawn from the language
user's [prior] knowledge of the person, objects, states of
affairs, or events the discourse is about.

That quiet observation logically discredits the policy of leaving language arts content chiefly to the tastes and leanings of
the individual child, especially in the early grades, before children can identify these for themselves. If you want children to
be good readers and learners, they need to know a lot about the
specific things that writers in a specific culture take for granted.
The most effective way to ensure that they know those things
is to offer them instruction in the background knowledge that
is most widely shared in newspapers, magazines, books, and
public conversations and is therefore going to be most needed
in their lives inside and outside school.

To understand a newspaper article about a baseball game, for
example, a reader has to know all kinds of facts not mentioned
in the piece: how many strikes put the batter out, whether
catching a fly ball puts the batter out, how many innings are
there in a game, and so forth.

Just in the past couple of years, this insight about the need
for specific background knowledge rather than general "reading comprehension skills" has taken the elementary-education
internet world by storm—a sign of tremendous progress. A
rediscovered 1988 article by Donna Recht and Lauren Leslie
marked the beginning of a kind of revolution in grasping the
need for a shared knowledge base in our elementary schooling.

The authors had gathered young students who had been tested as being either poor readers or good readers, and who had also been tested as having either high baseball knowledge or low baseball knowledge.

> Each subject silently read an account of a half inning of a baseball game. After reading, each subject recalled the account nonverbally by moving figures and verbally by retelling the story. After an interpolated task, they summarized the game and sorted passage sentences for idea importance. There was a significant main effect for prior knowledge on all measures. No interactions between prior knowledge and ability were found. These results delineate the powerful effect of prior knowledge.

Reading mastery is best gained by mastery of the words and shared knowledge of the culture. The same principle holds for science, math, the arts, and history. It's not enough to "think like a historian" or "think like a scientist."

The Need for Facts III: The Function of a Well-Furnished Long-Term Memory

There is currently great disparagement for learning "mere facts" in favor of "active curiosity" and other high-sounding terms. But your ability to flourish in a society depends on your ability to communicate, to put things together, solve problems effectively, and strategize effectively. And the more relevant knowledge you have in your long-term memory, the better you will succeed in real life.

There's a famous experiment that shows that problem solving is not a generic skill but is based on the knowledge that you bring to the problem. It also shows that the more knowledgeable you are, the faster and better you are at problem solving. What better way of proving this than observing chess players? There's no question about who is more of an expert at chess, the player who consistently wins or the player who consistently loses. And does the difference between winning and losing lie chiefly in knowing deep general principles and having an ability to think, or in knowing a lot of "mere facts"?

Herbert A. Simon, one of the giants of cognitive psychology, noticed an obscure PhD thesis that ultimately made its author a hero of the new science. Adriaan de Groot was a young doctoral student in psychology in the Netherlands who happened to be a very good chess player. For his doctoral dissertation (1946), he decided to analyze some of the elements of chess-playing skills. He must have been a rather charming young PhD student, considering that he persuaded the most eminent chess players to participate in his experiments: Paul Keres, Alexander Alekhine, Reuben Fine, Max Euwe, and Savielly Tartakower, as well as four masters, two women champions, a number of experts, and a range of amateurs, including various psychology professors and students. Chess is a particularly favorable subject for determining one's level of expertise, because its rankings are quite objective and precise. They are based on unimpeachable fact: who, on average, can beat whom.

The resulting book by De Groot in its 1965 translation— *Thought and Choice in Chess*—became famous. But, as in other cases of serendipity in science, it was *not* its analyses of chess players' thinking about game positions that made the book a milestone in psychology. Rather, what came to influence the field was a side experiment. It involved no strategic chess thinking at all: De Groot simply asked his subjects to reproduce on a blank board a midgame chess position that the subject had seen just for a few seconds. De Groot wanted to determine whether there was a correlation between a chess player's official ranking and the ability to reproduce accurately a midgame chess position.

Yes, there was an almost perfect correlation! The higher the player's rank from novice to grandmaster, the more pieces that were accurately reproduced. The lowest-ranked chess player could barely reproduce 30 percent of the pieces accurately, whereas a grandmaster was always able to reproduce accurately over 90 percent of them. De Groot postulated, quite correctly, as it proved, that this superior ability of the grandmasters did not depend on their having developed superior general skills, but rather on what he called their "erudition"—their encyclopedic knowledge of past games, which allowed them to quickly organize their perceptions into meaningful groupings that could then be reconstructed on a blank board.

This experiment ignited the interest of Simon, who with his colleague William Chase, took De Groot's work a step further. They asked the subjects to reproduce board arrangements that had a similar number of pieces (more than twenty) placed at random. These helter-skelter pieces were *not* in a midgame position from an actual game. In this new, contrived, experiment, *all the subjects—novices, masters, grandmasters—performed more or less the same.* They all reproduced correctly around six pieces. When it came to a brute memory task, equally novel to them all, they all performed as novices.

There is, then, no general chess-piece reproducing skill, no general mental muscle developed by playing hundreds of chess games. In real-game situations, the more erudite masters and grandmasters had a ready mental inventory of midgame positions based on their knowledge of past games. Simon and Chase ventured to estimate that their expertise derived from the stored memory of about fifty thousand chess games. It was ingrained, specific factual knowledge, stored in long-term memory, not some general mental skill, that explained the skilled performance.

But nobody holds fifty thousand chess games in long-term memory for quick retrieval. So there had to be a reason that the grandmasters possessed the ability to reproduce game positions and an ability to outstrategize their opponents consistently. It must be the case that the long-term memories of the grand-masters had organized their knowledge into *kinds* of situations and the individual situation of any particular game. Here's an excellent quick summary by the distinguished cognitive scientist Paul A. Kirschner and his associates:

Our understanding of the role of long-term memory in human cognition has altered dramatically over the past few decades. It is no longer conceived as a passive repository of discrete, isolated fragments of information that permit us to repeat what we have learned. Nor is it seen only as a component of human cognitive architecture that has merely peripheral influence on complex cognitive processes such as thinking and problem solving. Rather, long-term memory is now viewed as the central, dominant structure of human cognition. Everything we see, hear, and think about is critically dependent on and influenced by our long-term memory.

After citing De Groot's discovery and its subsequent expansion by Simon and Chase, and then several others, they sum up:

> We are skillful in an area because our long-term memory contains huge amounts of information concerning the area. . . . Without our huge store of information in long-term memory, we would be largely incapable of everything from simple acts such as crossing a street . . . [to] solving mathematical problems. Thus, our long-term memory incorporates a massive knowledge base that is central to all of our cognitively based activities. . . . The aim of all instruction is to alter long-term memory. If nothing has changed in long-term memory, nothing has been learned.

All this was summarized in Anders Ericsson's remark "There is no such thing as developing a general skill." The point applies to *all* school-learned activities and subject matters. It applies in spades to language use and reading comprehension.

It's a paradox that one of the most important educational insights in history, one with high currency in the world of cognitive psychology, should have arrived just at the time when the fad for twenty-first-century non–domain specific, non-existent skills should have reached a climax in the education world.

How the Brain Creates Shortcuts with Facts

We have come to understand at a rather basic level that brains can't *consciously* process very much information at any one time. This underlying principle helps explain at least in part why all skills are dependent on specific background knowledge. Skills depend on complex and fast processing, and that can be done only after *we have already coded a lot of complex knowledge in quickly available form*—as was the case with the erudite chess grandmasters.

From 1946 to 1970, psychologists conducted experiments in language whose results showed why shared background knowledge is key to language use. Given the memory limitations of the human brain, first analyzed decisively in 1956 by George A. Miller (another giant of psychology), it is impossible for us to say everything we need to say to make ourselves understood in conversation or on the page. If one does not manage to *imply* meaning, and do so quickly, the reader will lose the thread.

The limit of working memory permits just a few chunks to be held in mind at a time, before some of the chunks start dropping out in as little as a few seconds. That's the limit of what needs to be made meaningful and placed in our long-term memory store before we forget what we are hearing or reading. The constraints of working memory turn a normally good reader into a poor reader when the topic is unfamiliar.

For, as George A. Miller pointed out, the only way to overcome the severe limitations of working memory is to "chunk." That's what grandmasters did with past chess games. That's why the telephone companies group numbers into three chunks resembling words (226-487-2234) instead of nine digits that would be impossible to remember (2264872234). Then when the chunks are forwarded to our long-term memory, we can lodge them and retrieve them more or less permanently. This interchange between short-term memory and long-term memory is the basic structure of our mental life.

In language, more is always silently implied than what is explicitly said. But such implications can work only if both speaker and listener are on the same wavelength, which is an apt metaphor for "sharing the same knowledge and assumptions." To be on the same wavelength on the radio means that the station that is broadcasting the signal and the radio that is receiving it are both tuned to the same frequency for the same carrier signal.

Short-term memory is a stern disciplinarian. Its rules cannot be broken. It turns chess masters into novices when the domain is unfamiliar. George Miller discovered in his pathbreaking paper that the way to make short-term memory work effectively is to chunk, so that twenty-one pieces become six or fewer. The chess masters' well-stocked long-term memories enabled them to reproduce twenty-one pieces correctly so long as the chess positions in question were taken from actual games. A well-stocked, well-selected, well-practiced long-term memory is the secret of expertise.

Important educational implications clearly follow from this research. Note first that it refutes the familiar claim of American educators that you don't need to learn a lot of "mere facts," because you can always look them up on Google. Not so. Cognitive scientists have firmly established that you can't understand what Google is saying unless you already know a lot of the facts Google is assuming you know on the subject in question.

In another insightful article entitled "How Children Learn Words," George A. Miller and Patricia M. Gildea found that, in the absence of prior relevant knowledge, reference works like dictionaries and encyclopedias are often useless. For, in the absence of relevant, preexisting knowledge, the inferences that a person makes when consulting a reference work can be inadequate and distorting. He asked a group of children to look up some words and then use them in a sentence. Here are some examples:

> **CORRELATE:** "Me and my parents correlate, because without them I wouldn't be here."
> **METICULOUS:** "I was meticulous about falling off the cliff."
> **REDRESS:** "The redress for getting well when you're sick is staying in bed."
> **RELEGATE:** "I relegated my pen pal's letter to her house."
> **TENET:** "That news is very tenet."

So much for looking things up on Google if you are a fact-free novice. To explain the last example, Miller and Gildea exhibited the dictionary definition of tenet: "A principle, belief, or doctrine generally held to be true; especially: one held in common by members of an organization, movement, or profession." The child had grabbed hold of the word "true," applied the adjective, and came up with "That news is very true," which makes sense, whereas "That news is very tenet" is hilariously mysterious.

In light of now well-established scientific consensus, the principle of domain-specific knowledge as central to skills like critical thinking should be accepted by all rational people as truth. It demolishes the claim that our schools are teaching *all-purpose* skills like critical thinking through ad hoc child-chosen or teacher-chosen content. The general-skills myth has endured partly because it has enabled high officials to avoid the criticism and controversy that attends the actual specification of content. The persistence of the myth of critical thinking enables them to sidestep responsibility with a good conscience.

We need to let them know the emphatic scientific consensus. It is essential that the public demand specific grade-by-grade content in our elementary schools, so that one grade can build on another in a systematic way, a kind of schooling that is best for all students and especially beneficial to our least-advantaged students.

CHAPTER 6

The Lessons of Educational Failure and Success around the World

We have now seen how child-centered romanticism has caused American schoolchildren to slide downhill in their verbal scores. The same pattern has confounded other nations that have adopted child-centered romanticism. The "nature knows best" theory didn't start in the United States. Western Europe is the home of educational romanticism, with America its secondary residence. When American prestige rose after World War II, people in Europe began to think, "Maybe we should imitate the Americans."

In the late twentieth century, Germany, Sweden, and France experienced the same educational failures as in the United States, and from those same mistakes—though in two of those nations educational leaders were smart enough to rectify their errors and help their nations rise again nearer to the top. In Asia, China and Japan did not even momentarily experience such failures. They scorned the nineteenth-century romantic ideas about individualizing content in the classroom. As a result, schools in the Far East have continued to improve and now score at or near the top in international comparisons.

Germany and "PISA *Schock*"

Let's turn first to the German story, which is the most complete version of fall and redemption. In the year 2000, the Program for International Student Assessment (PISA) began issuing its comparative evaluations of the academic achievement of fifteen-year-old students from across the world. As we have seen, these PISA scores in reading, science, and math offer a quick snapshot of the quality of a national school system. Astonishingly, the German results of the first PISA test of 2000 were well *below* the international average in math, science, and reading. That was hugely embarrassing to a rich, advanced nation that was also the land of Leibniz, Kant, and Einstein. The German PISA results induced a national sense of crisis that the Germans called "PISA *Schock*." It produced a national soul searching. It caused the whole country to take a new look at romantic, naturalistic schooling—which it had invented, along with the "child garden."

Following this PISA *Schock*, the soul searching began, and the Länder (political divisions similar to US states) began to cooperate with one another. Before, each Land had issued its own vague standards. Now all of them decided to cooperate. Germany instituted what was in effect a shared-knowledge national curriculum in each grade of elementary school. After instituting this change, here is the pattern of their reading scores:

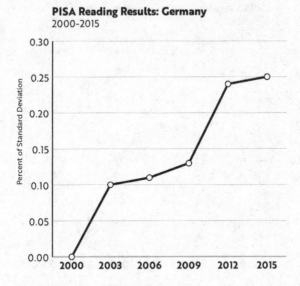

PISA Reading Results: Germany
2000-2015

The path still continues upward, and in recent results, Germany ranks tenth in the world, after having ranked twenty-second in 2000. (The United States currently ranks twenty-fourth; in 2000, the country ranked fifteenth!) There is no reason to doubt that US children would similarly start being more competent if the states began to follow the educational lead of the German Länder.

Let's turn now to a nation that did *not* interpret the PISA results accurately.

The Swedish Story

The Swedish story is equally informative in the other direction. Sweden changed from a shared-knowledge curriculum in its elementary schools to a constructivist orientation just

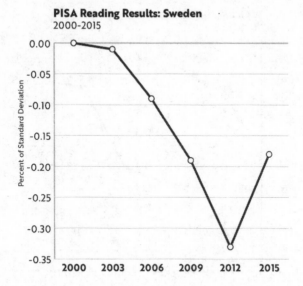

PISA Reading Results: Sweden
2000-2015

when Germany was going the other way. In 2000, Sweden ranked ninth in reading for fifteen-year-olds. In 2012, it ranked twenty-seventh.

The Swedish drop of over 30 percentile points between 2000 and 2012 is the largest drop so far recorded by PISA. The disastrous Swedish school reforms in 2000 featured a change from a shared curriculum in the early grades to a more localized, Americanized approach. That was precisely the opposite direction of the German reforms, and with the change came precisely the opposite results. But subsequently, Sweden, learning from its experience, has started moving back toward a shared-knowledge curriculum. Sweden thus performed its own scientific experiment on a big scale in the course of fifteen years. The results have trended sharply upward, and Sweden now ranks seventeenth. The steep downward descent after 2000, and the sharp upturn after 2012, is in line with the German results, and is commensurate with the positive results that are predicable after introducing a shared-knowledge curriculum. That prediction turns to a near certainty when we consider the example of France.

Here's What Happened to France When It Decided to Adopt Constructivist Ideas

These national data are scientifically more compelling than any contrived experiment could ever be, because of the large number of subjects sampled in the PISA scores. With millions of students represented in each nationwide sample, a lot of the potentially distorted variables in smaller experiments get completely washed out. Even a small effect can be quite significant. When the effects are huge, as in this case in France, the inferences become scientifically decisive.

That is particularly the case with France, whose national educational record-keeping is fuller and more exhaustive than that of most other nations. When all these different country-wide data point the same way in diverse nations, and when all of them are unfavorable to current American educational theory and practice, the inference is decisive, unless we evasively conclude that the French are different from Americans. But they seem to be pretty much the same: they have managed to achieve the same disastrous decline as we have—but even faster, and with very precise documentation, which we lack. So, let's look particularly closely at France.

In 1789 France had a bloody revolution that toppled kings;

in 1989 it had an educational revolution that knocked down its reputation as one of the most egalitarian nations in the world. Overnight, the educational revolution affected every city and rural village in France. Many millions of students were affected all at once.

Still, when the highly centralized French government de-centralizes one of its operations, it keeps detailed centralized records. Hence, we know with the precision of a controlled experiment the results of the change in each city, town, and village. France has unwittingly conducted the largest, most persuasive, and best-documented educational experiment in history.

For a hundred years before 1989, it used to be said that on any given day all schoolchildren in France in their respective grades would be studying the same story, math topic, and historical event. By a new national law in 1989, France's elementary schools were commanded to stop teaching a common curriculum and start teaching varied, American-style, personalized, "constructivist" curriculums that emphasized (nonexistent) general skills.

The vastness, radicalness, and suddenness of the change makes it possible to determine with high confidence the effects on students' competence of the two kinds of curricula. These effects manifested themselves in due course. Alarmed reports and books began to arrive with titles like: *The Destruction of the French Elementary School* (1998), *Et Vos Infants ne Sauront Pas Lire . . . (Your Children Won't Know How to Read or Add)* (2004), and *The Debacle of the School* (2007), all carrying the same apocalyptic tone as *A Nation at Risk*, and with similar justification.

The opportunity for studying before-and-after effects in

France is a great piece of luck for open-minded people. Every decade, France conducts a detailed nationwide study of the achievement levels of its fifth graders; the survey also includes demographic information about each tested student's family background. Not only was the 1989 change massive and universal, it was precisely monitored according to seven demographic and sociological categories. One such preschool-revolution survey had been conducted in 1987. That formed a baseline. The subsequent surveys in 1997 and 2007 used the identical tests as those administered in 1987. In effect, France conducted a nationwide, ongoing experiment with meticulous demographic data gathering.

But why would anyone have wanted to make such a radical change in France? The French school system was producing some of the best and most egalitarian reading scores in the world in the 1980s. The French record of social mobility was inspiring, with some of its most notable writers and politicians having risen from impoverished family circumstances as products of its highly egalitarian and meritocratic school system. The system began with its preschools, the famous *écoles maternelles*, and was followed by effective instruction under its national grade-by-grade elementary school curriculum.

We Americans were partly responsible for the decision to change. We had helped liberate France from the Germans in 1944. Our soldiers and generals marched through the streets of Paris as heroes. In the late 1960s, American prestige was still high. All things American—even Coca-Cola—were looked on with favor, and in French universities and teacher-training institutions, the educational ideas that had produced the victorious

Americans (or so it was assumed) began to catch on. The new constructivist ideas became the dernier cri in teacher-training institutions, taking hold first among young education professors, then gradually among the future teachers who gained their teaching certificates.

Then came the student protests in France in 1968. That too smacked of American influence. Remember what happened in Berkeley in the mid-1960s? By 1968, similar student protests were taking place at universities elsewhere in Europe, and especially in France. The most serious, government-threatening one occurred in Paris in May 1968, involving some twenty thousand protesters. It almost brought down General de Gaulle's government, which had to make concessions. One of these was an agreement to form a committee to formulate radical changes in French schooling.

A lot of the rioting students in 1968 had been born to immigrant parents from North Africa and the rural countryside. It was the French school system that had enabled them to enter the universities. They had arrived as fully qualified students, and were rioting from classes at France's best universities.

Who knows what causes student riots? But reasons about some unacceptable social situation are usually offered by the rioters. In this case, a precipitating element of the French riots of 1968 was a 1964 book about French education, *The Inheritors*, coauthored by Pierre Bourdieu and Jean-Claude Passeron. It became a casus belli for the students. A graduate of the École normale supérieure, Bourdieu, who became a famous sociologist, was raised by ill-educated parents from rural France who spoke a Gascon dialect at home. It was the French school system that enabled Bourdieu and other offspring of such families to fulfill their potential.

The book attacked the French school system for being insufficiently democratic. Bourdieu and Passeron claimed that the data showed that advantaged university students tended to choose elite majors like literature and history, whereas students from poorer homes chose majors like education or civil engineering. According to the authors, this showed that French schools perpetuated class structures. The book did not note that the children of these practical-minded, talented students who had chosen engineering might well produce children in confident, comfortable circumstances who would then choose literature as their major subject.

It was basically a silly book, but it gave the rioters a justification for their actions. By 1989, when the Socialists were in power, the book had already become a rallying point for a reform of the entire French school system, with Bourdieu named a leading member of the committee to advise the government on what the reforms should be. The committee's report recommended personalized education.

The oversight of the school curriculum was now to be under the control of each Département—of which there were ninety-six within France proper. Further, the report recommended, beyond that dispersal of curricular oversight, *each individual school was to choose its own special curricular focus.* And, further, each *student* was to be encouraged to choose his or her preferred topics and emphases. All this personalized freedom was meant to liberate students from the "rigidities" of a common curriculum. A law putting these recommended changes into immediate effect was passed by the national legislature.

When the French enthusiastically changed their schooling to the American style in the 1980s, they also experienced a similar precipitous decline shown here in percent of standard deviation: 80 percent in two decades! Thus, after two decades, there was a decline in French verbal scores of a magnitude similar to the huge decline in American verbal scores over *four* decades—and from the same intellectual causes.

French Average Verbal Scores
1987-2007

The achievement gap in France between rich and poor students then widened enormously. The following chart shows how different social classes were affected, a change that destroyed the formerly egalitarian nature of French education.

Even the decline in reading among midlevel professionals was over a full standard deviation.

It is a paradox that the intellectual *Left* in both France and the United States has instigated educational "reforms" that penalize the poor and favor the rich. Note too how much the overall gaps have widened between the top and bottom groups. This detailed sociological graph is a stunning sociological and moral indictment of our persisting in an incorrect educational theory.

French Reading Scores
1987-2007

No one disputes the commonsense verity that what children learn from the school curriculum affects their reading scores. At age thirteen, those scores chiefly measure the breadth of a student's background knowledge. A school curriculum that effectively and systematically imparts knowledge and thus narrows the knowledge gap will therefore narrow the reading test-score gap among groups. That equity effect of a coherent, knowledge-based curriculum is forcefully proved by the French experience.

But suppose the change in policy were to go the other way around than it did in France. Suppose the nation, using the same remarkable data gathering, had moved from an individualized, constructivist curriculum to a shared-knowledge curriculum such as France had in 1987. Suppose time ran backward in France. We'd get this picture:

Reversing the French (and American) Experience
2020-2037?

If we assume that the children of the unemployed and the laborers as a group in France might be comparable educationally to disadvantaged children in the United States, we can see that a coherent curriculum would induce an average improvement of about 40 percent, and a *narrowing of the black-white test-score gap of 60 percent*, which would be cause for fireworks and celebrations. We could declare victory in early education and turn our attention to another area of national concern. It would be a big leap forward toward giving every American child an equal chance, and it would help form a more competent and unified nation.

PART III

American Ethnicity: Will the Common School Make a Comeback?

CHAPTER 7

Commonality in a Multiethnic Nation

The Swiss may speak four languages and still act as one people, for each of them has enough learned habits, references, symbols, memories, patterns of landholding and social stratification, events in history, and personal associations, all of which together permit him to communicate more effectively with other Swiss than with the speakers of his own language who belong to other peoples.

—Karl W. Deutsch, *Nationalism and Social Communication* (1953)

A shared language says "We're the same." A language barrier says "We're different." The architects of apartheid understood this. Part of the effort to divide black people was to make sure we were separated not just physically but by language as well. The great thing about language is that you can just as easily use it to do the opposite: convince people that they are the same. Racism teaches us that we are different because of the color of our skin. But because racism is stupid, it's easily tricked. . . . If the person who doesn't look like you speaks like you, your brain short-circuits because your racism program has none of those instructions in the code. "Wait, wait," your mind says, "the racism code says if he doesn't look like me he isn't like me, but the language code says if he speaks like me he . . . is like me?"

—Trevor Noah, *Born a Crime* (2016)

The Common School Created America

The United States of America was the first big modern democracy, and along with Prussia the first society with free public schooling nationwide. It was Noah Webster's social aim from the start to create a "people" through schooling. If you look up world histories of education, you will find that the United States was the first in the modern era to introduce public schools at which children "of all ranks of society" would study the same things. In Europe and Asia, the names Noah Webster, Benjamin Rush, and Horace Mann are now praised as early exponents of the modern national school. Later generations of American teachers and principals shared that same nation-preserving goal. In the first century and a half of our national existence, we succeeded in creating a united citizenry based on a common language and common schooling.

Our early preference for common content was part of our urgent desire for national unity. At the founding, the watchword of every American patriot was "union." The first aim mentioned in the Constitution was to "form a more perfect union." It was a central theme in the formation of our federation of states. It had been a central theme in our debates over the Constitution. It was a continual theme of George Washington, Noah Webster, Alexander Hamilton, and James Madison in their speeches and writings. Throughout the young nation, streets were named "Union Avenue" and "Union Street," along with "Union Park" and "Union Square." It continued to be the theme of our most imposing political oratory—as in the ending of Daniel Webster's great speech of 1830: "Liberty and Union; now and forever: one and inseparable." When the Civil War came, the North, seeing itself as the protector of the American idea, called itself the "Union" as distinct from a "Confederacy."

Benjamin Franklin and Benjamin Rush from Pennsylvania, and Madison, Jefferson, and George Washington from Virginia believed that a mortal danger lay in our potential internal conflicts—Germans against English inside Pennsylvania, state against state, region against region, local interests against national interests, party against party, personal ambition against personal ambition, religion against religion, poor against rich, uneducated against educated. Unless controlled, these hostile "factions" would subvert the common good, breed demagogues, and finally turn the republic into a military dictatorship, just as in ancient Rome.

To keep that from happening, they believed we would need far more than the checks and balances described in the Constitution. We would also need a special new brand of citizen who, unlike the citizens of Rome and other failed republics, would subordinate his local interests to the common good. Unless we created this new and better kind of modern personality, we would not be able to preserve the republic.

Our early educators thought the school would be the institution that would transform future citizens into loyal Americans. It would teach common knowledge, virtues, ideals, language, and commitments. Benjamin Rush, a signer of the Declaration of Independence, wrote one of the most important early essays on American education. It advocated a common elementary curriculum for all. The paramount aim of the schools, he wrote, was to create "republican machines." By that he meant active, loyal, purposeful citizens of the republic.

George Washington bequeathed a portion of his estate to

education in order (he wrote) "to spread systematic ideas through all parts of this rising Empire, thereby to do away local attachments and State prejudices." Notice the emphasis on commonality—on welding the whole into a union, and citizens into a "people." Thomas Jefferson's plan for common schools every five miles aimed not only to secure the peace and safety of the republic but also to engender social fairness and to foster the best leaders. He outlined a system of elementary schooling that enabled all children, rich and poor, to go to the same school so that they would get an equal chance regardless of who their parents happened to be:

> Our plan prescribes the selection of the youths of genius
> from among the classes of the poor; we hope to avail the
> state of those talents which nature has sown as liberally
> among the poor as the rich.

As early as 1812, New York State passed the Common School Act, providing the basis for a statewide system of public elementary schools. In 1852 Massachusetts became the first state to make the common school compulsory for all children, and other states followed suit throughout the later nineteenth century. Such notions about the civic necessity of the common school animated American thinkers far into the nineteenth century.

The schools were to be supported by taxes and to have a common, statewide system of administration. And the early grades were to have a common core curriculum that would foster patriotism and solidarity. The aim was *not* just to assimilate the many immigrants then pouring into the nation but also to assimilate native-born Americans who came from different regions and social strata into the common language and the common American idea.

As early as 1825, the New York legislature established a fund to secure common textbooks for all of the state's elementary schools, specifying that

> the printing of large editions of such elementary works as the spelling book, an English dictionary, a grammar, a system of arithmetic, American history and biography, to be used in schools, and to be distributed gratuitously, or sold at cost.

The aim, they said, was *not* to

> make our children and youth either partisans in politics, or sectarians in religion; but to give them education, intelligence, sound principles, good moral habits, and a free and independent spirit; in short, to make them American free men and American citizens, and to qualify them to judge and choose for themselves in matters of politics, religion and government. . . . [By such means] education will nourish most, and the peace and harmony of society be best preserved.

These aims were actually met. They were not just pious slogans. We know this from the observations of an astute foreign observer. In the early nineteenth century, the French aristocrat and scholar Alexis de Tocqueville wrote a famous book about the new nation: *Democracy in America* (1835). He took special note of the aim of citizen making. How much more loyal to the common good Americans were than his quarrelsome fellow Europeans!

> It cannot be doubted that in the United States the education of the people powerfully contributes to the maintenance of the democratic republic. That will always be so, in my view, *wherever education to enlighten the mind is not separated from the education of civic duty.* [my italics] In the United States the general thrust of education is directed toward political life; in Europe its main aim is to fit men for private life. I concluded that both in America and in Europe men are liable to the same failings and exposed to the same evils as among ourselves in France. But upon examining the state of their society more attentively, I speedily discovered that the Americans had made great and successful efforts to counteract these imperfections of human nature and to correct the natural defects of democracy.

Such was the success of our school leaders and teachers in those cautious early days. (Of course. the exclusion of women from these comments rankles today.)

Nation creating was reinforced in our primers and spelling books on a scale never before seen in human history. Civil allegiance was to hold the society together, and reverence for the nation and its laws was to make it work. The new doctrine was no longer to be sectarian religion but devotion to democracy and reverence for its laws. The old religions were to be made less lethal by making them subject to civil law. Later in the nineteenth century, Lincoln wanted his patriotic, secular "reverence for the laws" to be the new civil religion. And the schools were to be secular pulpits that formed our diverse ethnic origins into a single American identity.

New York State, with its diversity of immigrants and religious affiliations, was especially alert to the need to build up a shared public sphere where all these different groups could meet as equals on common ground. It's illuminating to read the worried but hopeful speeches of its state education superintendents and governors in the early and mid-nineteenth century. Like Madison and Lincoln, they understood that the American political experiment, which respected everyone's autonomy in the private sphere, depended on a vigorous public sphere that only the schools and newspapers could create. Those early speeches are filled with cautionary references to the South American republics that were then collapsing into military dictatorships. Unless our schools created Americans, they warned, that would be our fate. Governor Silas Wright said in his address to the New York legislature in 1845:

On the careful cultivation in our schools, of the minds of the young, the entire success or the absolute failure of the great experiment of self-government is wholly dependent; and unless that cultivation is increased, and made more effective than it has yet been, the conviction is solemnly impressed by the signs of the times, that the American Union, now the asylum of the oppressed and "the home of the free," will ere long share the melancholy fate of every former attempt of self-government. That Union is and must be sustained by the moral and intellectual powers of

the community, and every other power is wholly ineffec-
tual. Physical force may generate hatred, fear and repul-
sion; but can never produce Union. The only salvation for
the republic is to be sought for in our schools.

It's the premise of this book that Silas Wright, like Noah
Webster, was precisely correct. Their worry about unity was
justified. Today, every political poll indicates that most Americans believe the country is headed in the wrong direction—in
many domains. The decline of patriotism is palpable. Earlier,
I described how our schools persist in the blithe tradition of
child-centered progressivism, which took over the thought
world of our teacher-training institutes. How prescient the
founders were in being worried about factions and lack of public spirit and even disloyalty to the republic. We have, to our
distress, acquired some of the evils they feared.

Moreover, the decline of shared knowledge and ideals leads
to factions and to incompetence—or as we say these days, to
"polarization." And—as we don't like to admit—it leads to a
dumbing-down of our people, according to objective criteria
like the PISA results.

Why Did We Abandon Commonality?

By the 1930s and 1940s, our great success as a nation had made
us overconfident and overly optimistic. We no longer worried
about the precariousness of republican government. We believed that mankind was marching onward, with us in the lead.
It's useful to watch that March of Time movie-short about progressive education in the 1940s. The footage of John Dewey

telling the audience that we are not preparing our children for our world but theirs is especially emblematic. Dewey was a highly sophisticated philosopher, but also a believer in the premise that to follow nature is to progress onward and upward. In that, he expressed the dominant American optimism of the 1930s and 1940s—and beyond.

Our teacher-training institutes, as I have explained, have remained faithful to the idea that society will flourish if nature in the form of the child's natural development is allowed to take its providential course. As we now know, nature does not want us humans to take its "providential course," because it has given us a blank slate rather than a blueprint. It wants us to act as our American founders did, with a knowledge-drenched caution, based on the sad history of earlier republics. In the 1930s we ceased thinking of nature as red in tooth and claw, and we lost our founders' acute sense of tragedy and danger. We can no longer watch helplessly our palpable decline. It is time to act intelligently on the insights of history as did our founders, now supplemented by the insights of science.

True proficiency of language is an expertise that every single American deserves to have—a proficiency that opens up all sorts of opportunities that are otherwise closed, including an opportunity to run for political office. No person is going to be nominated or elected who doesn't talk the talk and understand the talk. Nobody is going to be accepted at a good college who doesn't do well on the verbal section of a college entrance exam. In the public sphere, even the most poorly educated Americans want to understand what is being said. They want their public speakers to use the formal language of radio, television, and the speaker's lectern. And shared language requires shared knowledge. A renewed increase of commonality in American elementary schools would make American life better and more productive, and do so without turning people into conformist robots. This idea may feel initially disorienting, given the power of our Emersonian-style romantic individualism, but shared language and knowledge doesn't suppress individuality; rather, it enables greater competence. Once knowledge becomes shared, it becomes naturalized in the same way that immigrants who have earned their citizenships then belong to the federated whole.

Modern life has overtaken provincial education, at least in the domain of language and knowledge. No matter what state or city an American child lives in, he or she deserves to gain full mastery of Standard American English. It's the language that everyone speaks in the public sphere. It has no special group attached to it. It is the language that announces: "I'm just as good as you. And you are just as good as I am. We are equal." It is the key to success and personal fulfillment. It has to be taught deliberately and effectively. Also essential to language competence is silently shared knowledge that may not appear on the surface but is the decisive feature of a shared identity.

Updating the Common School: Diversity

"Diversity" is a big theme in current debates about American schooling. There is an understandable demand to include in the school curriculum more representation of African American and Hispanic culture and people, along with greater representation of women, gays, and other neglected or formerly disrespected Americans. This is an easy and desirable demand to put into effect. As with other parts of a shared-knowledge curriculum, the key issue is the integration of these perspectives into the common curriculum. Knowledge is not functional in language and culture until it is shared. Hence the key practical matter to settle is determining which are the specific elements of knowledge about African Americans, Hispanics, and other minorities that need to be shared going forward.

In general, we need to answer another, similar practical question: What are the specific elements of the *traditional* shared knowledge of the nation, grade by grade, that we need to share along with this new material? In the current pedagogy of American elementary education, the requirement of specific topics is a nearly untouchable concept except in the uncontroversial subject of mathematics. Trying to get nationwide or statewide or even district or schoolwide agreement about specific grade-by-grade subject matter in history, literature, or the arts is like touching some poisonous object. But there are worse things than being criticized, if as a consequence of noncommonality poor children become even more disadvantaged and one's country performs at a mediocre level.

The solution now lies mainly with the public; opposition seems too entrenched among many of our education professionals. Those few rebels who demand a movement away from child-centered education need to be supported by parents and patriots. The public should make the need for a common curriculum *more* threatening to the jobs of controversy-averse education officials than any conceivable gripe about a choice of particular content. Then, if members of the public do raise their voices, they also have an obligation to support any official who has the courage to require grade-by-grade specificity of school topics. Any officials who do have that courage will raise children's abilities and make their community far abler than before.

If we do not want to fragment ourselves, if we want America to be unified and productive, we will ensure that our inherent diversity is embraced by a genuine unity of knowledge and sentiment. The two realities do not exclude each other; they did not during much of our past, and we must not allow intellectual and emotional confusion to fragment us now.

Updating the Common School: Globalism

"Nationalism" gets a negative rap because it is identified with people who dislike immigrants and scorn citizens of other nationalities, and also because people associate the term with deplorable "white nationalism." But there are sound practical reasons for democracies to focus their attention on the well-being of their nation while still engaged in cooperative internationalism. In his preface to the second edition of his great book on nationalism, Karl Deutsch (who participated in the creation of the United Nations) observed that he had little to change in his earlier book, because the nation-state is the social arrangement that gets things done. International cooperation has become essential. But so far, the evidence is that international groupings like the European Union have not replaced the nation-state, and they do not seem destined to do so. The evidence indicates that the modern nation-state will remain for a very long time the ultimate limit of human *social* organization, as the sociologist Émile Durkheim stated in a 1910 lecture to schoolteachers:

For the teaching of morality to be possible, the notion of society must be kept intact. It must be maintained that society is the very precondition of civilization and humanity. And since the nation is nothing other than the most highly organized society, you can see that to deny the nation is not simply to deny her received ideas; it is to deny the moral life at its very source. No doubt, we believe that we can counterpoise the fatherland with humanity in general. That is a huge mistake. The most highly constituted group, the highest that exists, is the political society, the fatherland, the *patria.*

I haven't seen anything in recent history to contravene that sociological insight. In fact, the most recent empire in history is a textbook case for the unstable society of the multilingual empire—the Soviet Union. It had its common currency, but it could not swallow Ukraine, much less Latvia and Lithuania, each with an established print language perpetuated in elementary schools. The post-Gutenberg era of standardized national print languages has revealed those print languages and national cultures to be stubbornly persistent. Even under suppression, modern print languages have preserved vast communication networks.

But Durkheim was thinking beyond the purely technical difficulty of unifying a multilingual nation. Switzerland, though small, had already shown that plural languages alone do not make nationwide social unity impossible. The difficulty in the Soviet Union was that, unlike Switzerland, it lacked a unity of shared knowledge and value. Quite the contrary: the Soviet Union was patched together under coercion without shared knowledge and values. Similarly, the European Union, while sharing some common values including a devotion to democracy and to peace and to economic integration, is nowhere near what Durkheim would call a "society." There are enormous shared-knowledge-and-value disjunctions within the European Union, whereas in Switzerland, many an individual Swiss is a member of an army whose members stand ready to die in defense of their homeland even if the attacking force has invaded a canton they do not live in, and one whose inhabitants speak a language they do not. That kind of devotion and loyalty is not to be found in the European Union. And in fact, the EU exhibits uneasy tensions among some of its members. In short, globalism, the idea that "our one world is one nation," lacks the cultural and emotional unity that could promise permanence.

What about the United States? Do we in our multicultural country have the ability to come together as citizens? But before I discuss that key issue, I need to address the more nitty-gritty practical issue of how we in the United States might solve the currently resistant problem of how our elementary schools might once again be brought to teach shared, value-laden knowledge, which is, as Durkheim and Deutsch wisely say, the essential underpinning of unity in any society.

CHAPTER 8

How to Improve the "Common Core"

Praise is due to those energetic reformers who have brought the Common Core State Standards into existence. The thought leaders, philanthropists, and governors who have created and supported the initiative are public benefactors to whom, if the standards get some concrete content, we will owe high gratitude. It took imagination and salesmanship to get the basic idea of commonality accepted by so many states. And once these multistate standards put flesh on their bones and manage to achieve their proper form, they will mark a permanent change for the better in our schools and country.

But the Common Core standards have not yet raised our students' scores in language, math, and science, nor have they narrowed the gaps between advantaged and disadvantaged students. Its advocates acknowledge that failure but say: "It's the early days. These things take time." That's true. But the *main* reason the standards have not had much effect on outcomes is that they are not yet specific. They lack content, and only specific content can induce the shared knowledge needed to sustain a nation.

What's needed can be understood by reminding ourselves of

the constraints of a classroom. Here are twenty young students. They can't reliably learn about multiplication until they have already learned about addition. If some students in the class have no understanding of addition, that will slow down every-one else, as time is then taken in order to explain addition. Alternatively, the class could forge ahead without pause, and the children who need help with addition could be placed in a re-medial class; or they could stay for after-school tutoring, which is costly. More likely, they would sit in the class, fall further be-hind, become frustrated, and create some behavioral problems. Or the teacher could slow down the whole class while addition is reexplained, a practice that is boring to the better-informed students. It's never possible in a mixed class to overcome bore-dom *entirely*. But it's desirable to reduce boredom by ensuring that all students enter the class knowing addition.

How can we do that? We can create specific standards, so each classroom becomes a speech community whose mem-bers all understand what is being said, because they all possess the needed relevant background knowledge. Every subject of schooling is language dependent—even art history, math, and engineering. And, in fact, even *those* subjects get encoded in our minds in quasilinguistic or symbolic form. Much of our think-ing is coded symbolically in the neocortex, and those symbols can be translated into words. But we cannot understand the words of the classroom unless we have the silently assumed knowledge to do so.

Once this fundamental truth is understood regarding the critical need of prior background knowledge to understand *any* speech transaction, then the necessary structure of all good classroom topic-standards—not just in arithmetic—comes clearly into focus. Topics cannot be randomly chosen but must be seeded beforehand. Such careful sequencing cannot readily be accomplished by a diversity of topics in the same classroom.

A good elementary curriculum in any school, district, or nation *must* therefore exhibit three criteria to have a truly significant effect on the quality and equity of schooling. *Coherence* over time is essential for ensuring that all students have the needed background knowledge for cumulative learning; *commonality* is essential to ensure inclusion of everyone and the forming of the classroom into a speech community; and *specificity* is necessary to ensure commonality. Data from around the world confirm that these three criteria are essential to producing excellent and equitable results.

But these qualities are not yet elements of the Common Core State Standards. This means that despite their admirable goals and despite the admirable efforts by the Gates Foundation and others to put them into effect in a constructive way, improvements are needed, especially in the key early grades K–6. The different subject matters need to be integrated into a coherent experience within the year and over the years. The whole of the curriculum needs to be kept in view, making it cumulative and coherent and specific.

On those criteria, let's consult the best-performing nations in the PISA rankings to see if they illustrate the point. We'll start with Singapore—an obvious move, since that country has been number one in the PISA rankings in all three of the PISA subjects: reading, math, and science.

Singapore, with a population of 5.6 million, educates as many pupils as do a majority of the individual states of our union, each of which, under our Constitution, has control of the state school curriculum. Never mind that Singapore is a multiracial, multicultural country that must be doing something right in its primary schools. So let's see what's in its curriculum guide for elementary school.

Singapore's introductory document for the elementary grades turns out to be a marvelous description of an ideal elementary education, one that strikes a balance of content mastery, skills, and values. It is well written, and it even offers a special word of praise for John Dewey! To get more detail on what exactly is in the curriculum, one needs to go to Singapore's approved textbook list. There one finds the entire list of approved books for the early grades, all published by Marshall Cavendish Education. Here's the language proficiency series:

- *Character and Citizenship Education* 1 through 6 (activity books and textbooks for each level). In Singapore, "language arts" is called "character and citizenship education." The terminology is very clear about the formative, acculturative character of shared language and shared knowledge—a much more sophisticated and accurate approach than our "language arts," whose title implies that language proficiency is a set of abstract skills. Rightly understood, language proficiency is a social art inherently connected to society. It holds a given society together, and it is intimately connected to what Durkheim called *moralité*, which can very accurately be translated as "character and citizenship education."

- *My Pals Are Here! Science 3&4 and 5&6* (Textbooks: *Cycles, Diversity, Interactions, and Systems*; workbook: *Systems*) For science, Singaporean children read a series called *My Pals Are Here! Science*, described as follows: "Each grade level consists of two parts, an A and a B set. Rather than chopping up the different branches of science into different grade levels and books, a thematic approach is taken, where concepts from different areas of science, including life science, physical science, chemistry, and physical science are all linked together. This approach is meant to help children think about the relationships between different science concepts to lead to a more complete understanding of our world."

- *Inquiring into Our World* (Pupil's Folio and Activity Books) For social studies, the *Inquiring into Our World* series is "designed to prepare pupils to be citizens of tomorrow helping them to better understand the world they live in and appreciate the complexities of the human experience." It also seeks to instill in pupils a deeper understanding of the "values that define Singaporean society, and to nurture their dispositions to show concern for the world they live in and demonstrate empathy in their relationships with others." This is hardly a just-the-facts approach. It's deliberately acculturative and patriotic.

The coherence and specificity of the Singaporean elementary schools are guaranteed by a simple administrative device: "You must teach *this single textbook and its coherent and specific content*." Singapore does not *need* to publish an elaborate guide to content. It simply mandates one single well-crafted series of year-by-year textbooks from which every schoolchild in the country must be taught. *Their* common core is totally specific and cumulative in content, which the publisher, Marshall Cavendish Education, arrived at after a lot of study and wide consultation. Whether each student in the class has the prior knowledge needed to understand the lesson is not factored into the equation.

Here's a bit of a contrast. American educational publishers advertise for writers on websites like Craigslist and freelance job boards. One freelance writer, John Riddle, describes it this way in *Writers Weekly*:

I came across an ad online about 15 years ago. They were looking for multiple writers for multiple projects. That certainly got my attention and I responded right away with some brief information about myself as a writer, and links to some of my published works.

Within only a few hours, I received a reply from an editor at Mason Crest Publishing, which was about to launch a new American history series. They gave me a choice of three titles to choose from: "The Story of the Pony Express," "Famous Forts," or "Famous Indian Battles." I felt as if I was playing a round of Jeopardy, and I replied, "I'll take the Pony Express for two thousand dollars, please." . . .

Within a few months, other work-for-hire book projects were being offered to me! Rates ranged from $750 to $3,500 per project. I could not believe how easy it was to write for those publishers.

Sometimes these books are vetted by subject-matter experts or teachers; some publishers don't take that step. What we're left with are quickly produced books filled with errors and omissions, and rather than spending the money to perfect a small number of books, publishers have found it more profitable to keep churning out new ones each year.

With the financial motivations of the educational companies and the unwillingness of government leaders to do anything to impose an explicit plan for education, how could *we* ever achieve the high degree of coherence and specificity necessary for technical excellence and fairness—two outstanding qualities of Singaporean education?

What we need is for each US state or a coalition of states to create a *specific grade-by-grade topic sequence.* That is essential for good and fair elementary schooling. Any other approach (no matter how politically and commercially attractive) is inferior in principle. We should not accept inferior educational principles just because they are politically and commercially convenient. Nor should we pretend that inferior principles are superior ones. To be fair, our educators have been following inferior principles partly because the progressive traditions that we have inherited from the first half of the twentieth century, though incorrect, are still earnestly adhered to. To make their standards grade-and-topic specific is the still-to-be-accomplished task of the Common Core State Standards.

In response to the widely heard claim that mandating specific statewide or nationwide topics will lead to thought control, parents and other citizens should respond that broad knowledge leads to *less* danger of thought control. The technical reason that Singapore now scores at the top in reading, math, and science is that Singaporean students *know* more than students in other countries. That's hardly thought control.

Broad knowledge is widely and democratically spread among all Singaporean students. A purely random group of its fifteen-year-olds will perform splendidly in reading, math, and science—no matter the educational and economic level of their parents and caregivers. The average Singaporean students know a lot because their schools have imparted knowledge very effectively to all.

The most important statement in the Common Core State Standards has to do with the need for implementing a "content rich" curriculum. But as we saw in the case of Singapore, if you have a content-rich curriculum, you don't need "standards." Indeed, as teachers have earnestly told me, if you just have "standards," you can teach pretty much any content you like.

In the current language arts standards, much of the technical detail about "complexity" and "genre" can be completely ignored. Textual complexity is not a scientifically valid criterion, because textual complexity may be quite easy to the student when the subject matter is familiar, and textual simplicity quite difficult when the subject matter is unfamiliar. The criterion is adopted because *something* had to be specified in the Common Core State Standards. Unfortunately, that kind of empty standard reinforces the mistake our schools made when the progressive tradition changed the verbal subject itself to "language arts." The terms "complexity" and "genre" imply the same fallacy about skills— the skill of reading complex texts; the skill of reading novels; the skill of reading lyric poetry. But we now know that these don't exist as content-independent general skills.

If a "content rich" common curriculum is put into effect

intelligently, students will master needed skills in the course of mastering the demands of a challenging, coherent curriculum. The superior verbal skills demonstrated by American students on the SAT verbal test back in 1952 owed to their having more of the shared knowledge needed for social communication than the students of 2012. That, not our lack of nonexistent abstract skills, explains the decline of our scores.

Reaching Agreement in the United States

The argument for topic commonality as the basis for excellence in early schooling has everything going for it technically: science, data, proof of concept. It lacks only the adherence of those who administer our schools, and who have been trained under the late-twentieth-century tradition of romantic individualism. Those who administer our schools under constructivist principles and those who teach in them deeply desire what is best for our children and our nation. What we need is a plan for persuading them to take a new direction. It's possible that the Common Core initiative can offer such an opportunity.

A group of respectable nonpolitical organizations would need to come together to create a set of very explicit topic sequences in all the subjects to be taught in elementary school. They would take advantage of the internet and put some model grade-by-grade textbooks online, along with useful instructional guides for teachers that could also be printed out for free. The results would be the best proof of success. The schools that used such an explicit, integrated approach would flourish. The children would be highly enthusiastic. Their reading scores would shoot up. The eighth-grade graduates would be admitted

tive high schools, for which they would have to pass on exams. They would become knowledgeable citizens, regardless of their original backgrounds.

It's a free country. Nothing should prevent this from happening if the desire is there to make it happen. Maybe there's a state governor somewhere who could manage to win public backing to carry out such an initiative. When her state started surpassing all the others in equity and level of achievement, the common school might finally make a comeback.

A True-Life Story

In Charlottesville, Virginia, in 1990, at the end of a conference of some one hundred people, hope was high. The conference had been called to improve and then ratify a content sequence for the elementary grades. Scholars, teachers, administrators, heads of associations, and subject-matter experts from all over the nation had come together to put the finishing touches on a provisional sequence for grades K–6 that had been sent out as a draft in advance. The draft had been previously reviewed by three separate groups of teachers across the country. The plan was to divide the attendees into working groups of ten, each with the job of putting the final touches on a grade level or a subject area.

How had we reached that point? Some initial preparatory work had been done over the prior three years, when professors Joseph Kett and James Trefil and I worked out a master list of topics and words that should be known to literate Americans. That had formed the basis of the cultural literacy list of 1987, and then of the more topically organized list for the *Dictionary of Cultural Literacy* of 1988. It made sense that this nonspecialist knowledge base of educated Americans could serve as a start. Then it could be broken down into topics that might belong exclusively to high school and college.

What remained was a version that focused on what children needed to know by the end of grade six. We asked experienced teachers from all over the nation to break down that list by grade, kindergarten through sixth. Now, over three days at the Boar's Head Inn, we worked with participants of different political and pedagogical persuasions who had started out highly suspicious of one another but now had become persuaded of their mutual goodwill and patriotism.

There were ten working groups and five sessions. The groups worked on committees whose membership shifted in each of three sessions per day. Each working group had been given full power to add or delete topics with regard to a particular grade level. The only rule was to take into account the teachers and students who would be using the programs. If you put a topic in, you had to remove an equally time-consuming topic. At the end of each working day, the changes were discussed and ratified by the conference as a whole. We had just unanimously ratified the last changes and were ready to close shop.

At the final session of the conference, a very sympathetic-looking gentleman came up to the podium and asked the chair (me) if he could address a few words to the conference. Of course! He introduced himself to the group as Paul Bell, superintendent of schools for Miami-Dade County, a huge and highly diverse school district, and the fourth-most-populous district in the nation.

He began by complimenting the group for what we had accomplished. He said that this sequence was going to be put into full effect in the schools of Miami-Dade within two years, with the initial implementation to begin the very next school year; that the parents and teachers in his district were hungry for this kind of coherent approach to substance; that they were tired of empty, skill-centered preparation for tests. He said he did not care what the initial tests results would say, because he knew, and he would make it clear to his teachers and parents, that this approach would ultimately make the key difference for all students.

Bell got an immediate standing ovation. I still get teary, though, when I think about Dade and Paul Bell. He went at it too hard, and three months later he was dead of a heart attack at age fifty-seven. And I still think of that unique pioneering effort by someone in high authority as a lost chance for our public schooling, and as the most tragic disappointment of my long journey in educational reform.

Paul would have prevailed. He was a powerfully magnetic person who knew the ropes. He had come up through the ranks as a teacher in Miami-Dade County. The results in the county would have shown up in the high school results and the National Assessment of Educational Progress. The United States would have taken notice, and perhaps we would have become unstuck much earlier from our failing schools.

The topic list that Paul was working to implement became the Core Knowledge Sequence, a grade-by-grade curriculum guide for some two thousand schools all over the country, including some whose successes I have described in this book. A part of the sequence is in use in some four thousand schools that follow the Core Knowledge English Language Arts program.

If a state now decided to put similar coherence and specificity into the Common Core and create a "content rich" curriculum that the Common Core demands, it would probably do a more authoritative and politically acceptable job than we managed at the Boar's Head Inn in 1990. But the theoretical premises wouldn't be any better. There is a necessary logic to making the content of a society's early schooling coincide with the already-shared knowledge and values of competent people in that society. And just as the completely open process at the Boar's Head Inn turned a very diverse and initially skeptical group into colleagues at the end, so would a similar process initiated by one or more states ultimately be received favorably.

The resulting curriculum should offer a topic sequence for the *whole of the elementary curriculum*, not just language arts or some other subject. Canada, which is tied for second place in the PISA rankings in reading, makes it clear that language arts is not a separate skill. To think of literature in that way is not far from what Horace Mann was getting at in his reports about forming our early public schools in Massachusetts. Our hypothetical forward-looking state would be wise to follow suit, and to abandon the now-known-to-be-incorrect premise that language proficiency is a natural, inborn skill. It is a knowledge-drenched skill. Each utterance, to be understood, requires specific, unstated background information.

Conclusion: Who Decides Such a Curriculum?

The evidence shows that helter-skelter content based on the child's interests leads to low verbal scores and low levels of educational equity, and that common content leads to high verbal scores and high equity. That is a statement that no scientifically informed person will challenge. So is there perhaps some powerful moral or social argument that makes the child-centered helter-skelter approach nonetheless seem preferable to forming a topic-specific curriculum? What then *are* the counterarguments?

Here are the ones that I have found:

Common content will lead to

thought control,

political control,

deprivation of freedom of choice,

lockstep uniformity, and

loss of independence and inventiveness.

That's the tenor of the current objections. Common content will lead to the possibility of a dictator or group taking over America; a decline of inventiveness; the neglect of some children; everyone thinking alike; and a loss of freedom by the American population. There is a distinct lack of evidence for these negative predictions. Did any of these things happen earlier when our schools deliberately taught common content? Quite the contrary.

I was born in 1928. I went to elementary school in the early 1930s, before the new wave of romanticism had reached as far as Memphis, Tennessee. The curriculum that I received was nation centered, not child centered. We learned US history. We honored the American founders. We learned by heart the preambles to the Declaration of Independence and the Constitution. We learned about the Civil War. We memorized not only the Pledge of Allegiance and the "Star-Spangled Banner," but also the Gettysburg Address. We learned the parts of speech.

My generation experienced elementary public schooling that was more or less the same across the land. We were all like the major general in Gilbert and Sullivan, who knew the kings of England and could quote the facts historical from Marathon to Waterloo in order categorical, except that we knew the presidents instead of the kings of England. We knew lots of "useless" facts. Yet for us in the 1930s and 1940s, all that "useless" shared knowledge did turn us into quite good *readers*. And in my case, while being brought up in the stifling racism of Memphis, Tennessee, it enabled me to read *An American Dilemma* by Gunnar Myrdal, which opened my eyes and allowed me to *escape* the dominant prejudices around me. That is, it enabled just the opposite of thought control!

It was my generation and those just before and after who led the civil rights movement. That was Martin Luther King Jr.'s education too. In high school he was raised on Baker and Thorndike or the equivalent. He knew which buttons to push, because our "mere fact" education had supplied most Americans with those same buttons. Our average verbal scores were in the top group in international rankings. How else can such a massive change for the better as the civil rights movement be accomplished except by people who are intellectually and socially competent?

But as the United States' verbal scores have declined, it has become ever easier for a demagogue to lead us sheep-like against other sheep-like followers. The demonization of the other in our politics is the result of ignorance, and of living by slogan. The patriotic, thoughtful vital center shrinks. Am I saying that a knowledge-rich national curriculum would produce a powerful, vital political center? Yes.

Defenders of the status quo often ask *who* should decide what we should all know. That is supposed to be a conversation stopper. The unexceptionable answer would be: "The majority should decide, as is normal in a democracy." But perhaps that's not what "who decides?" actually means. Perhaps it means: "What group of experts *should* have the power to choose the content? Why should we trust any single small elite group with such power? Doesn't that raise the specter of thought control?" No, so long as the process and the results are fully public.

Whatever the concrete topic sequence determined by whatever patriotic and savvy group, any city or state that adopted a well-thought-out topic-specific K–8 curriculum and classroom materials would begin topping the charts in achievement and equity. Elsewhere, the public would demand to follow suit, especially when none of the supposed evil consequences of commonality appeared. The public uproar that would be raised would be against those who declined to impose a shared-knowledge curriculum.

Public support for this kind of transformative educational agenda would be essential. Teachers who needed special content training would get the support they need. The first requirement for good teaching at every level is knowledge of the specific subject, not knowledge of pedagogical technique. The second-most-valuable teacher-training element is advice from experienced teachers about particular approaches that have worked well with *that* topic for *each specific* age group. Such training would immediately help ensure competent teaching and be likely to meet with parental as well as teacher approval.

And the plan would win over many teachers. Not only would they be given more adequate training and support materials, but they also would have an emotional stake in the positive outcome for their state and country. On the basis of the historical and scientific evidence, the results would be overwhelmingly positive for their communities, and all parents would demand that their children be offered such a chance. (That parental demand is what happens by the thousands every year with Jeffrey Litt's schools in the South Bronx.)

The results and the logic will prove inescapable. People elsewhere in the nation will conclude that much of the content sequence should be concrete and shared in their states as well. The tired slogans used against commonality and content specificity will lose their hold. They will be seen as reactionary, not forward looking. And gradually not only enthusiastic parents but more satisfied and competent students will prevail. The change will be overwhelmingly positive for our children and the country as a whole.

It will be a long slog. But the French have an apt saying: "The long distance is nothing. The first step is what's hard."

CHAPTER 9

Patriotism

Shared Knowledge and Kindness

Let reverence for the laws, be breathed by every American mother, to the lisping babe, that prattles on her lap—let it be taught in schools, in seminaries, and in colleges; let it be written in Primers, spelling books, and in Almanacs;—let it be preached from the pulpit, proclaimed in legislative halls, and enforced in courts of justice. And, in short, let it become the political religion of the nation; and let the old and the young, the rich and the poor, the grave and the gay, of all sexes and tongues, and colors and conditions, sacrifice unceasingly upon its altars.

—Abraham Lincoln, Lyceum Address (1838)

A Note on Kindness (adj. etymology): "friendly, deliberately doing good to others," Middle English kinde, from Old English (ge)cynde "natural, native, innate," originally "with the feeling of relatives for each other." Hence "kindness" is understood an ungendered, etymologically correct translation of "fraternité or brotherhood," as in liberté, égalité, fraternité, the great battle cry of the French Revolution.

Yes, we teach patriotism. We recite the Pledge of Allegiance every morning, and we constantly urge the children to be kind to everybody no matter where they came from. That's the essence of patriotism.

—Sheila Durant, principal of PS 69, the highest-scoring
regular public school in the South Bronx

"Nationalism" and "Patriotism" Are Not Dirty Words

Those who make a facile distinction between patriotism and nationalism (claiming the first means love, the other hate) have distorted two perfectly good words. Nationalism and patriotism both have the same root meaning: loyalty to one's birthland (*natio*) and one's fatherland (*patria*); loyalty to one's parents, including one's tribe. This elemental and widespread concept has an evolutionary benefit, because the cooperative social group has a better chance of surviving than does the individual. Education in a society aims to create not just smarter, happier kids, but above all, a better, more durable society.

Émile Durkheim, whose writings have powerfully influenced this book, was probably right to say that the modern nation-state is the largest, most stable *social* unit of humankind and our most potent source of morality and social unity. The benefit of bigness in a social group is safety and prosperity. If your group is large and powerful, few will attack you. In modern times, national print languages have helped unite large national populations. Those print languages and the shared public cultures learned in elementary school make us *feel* that we are comembers of a society. Without that bond, we tend to feel quite the opposite.

The Pledge of Allegiance is no longer recited in some public schools. Unfortunately, American patriotism has fallen into disrepute among some Americans who do not want to impose our culture on the cultures and ethnicities of nonnative citizens. Patriotism has become unfashionable for that and other high-minded reasons, including being repelled by narrow, jingoistic forms of group loyalty. But people who feel this concern for nonnative citizens have *essentialized* ethnicity. They have failed to understand the enormous power and validity of the American idea of a deliberately conceived unity and ethnicity.

Our civil religion, with the Declaration and Constitution as our bible, is nonsectarian. But as Durkheim profoundly saw, it needs to carry absolute religious authority. Our early schoolmasters understood the imperative of God-inspired patriotism. They instituted the Pledge of Allegiance to the American flag as a daily quasireligious morning ceremony of the elementary school. The nineteenth-century author of the Pledge of Allegiance, Francis Bellamy, was an idealistic Socialist who had the moral imagination to add a very abstract moral concept to the child's idea of personal loyalty to the flag and to the republic for which it stands—a little civics lesson in the middle of the school ritual. The educational historian Diane Ravitch describes the pledge as part of our former school practices and civil religion:

Until the last generation, American public schools took the teaching of patriotism very seriously. The school day began with the Pledge of Allegiance, every classroom displayed an American flag, the flag was raised each day over the school, and students learned the songs of the American civil religion—the national anthem, "God Bless America," "Columbia, the Gem of the Ocean," "America the Beautiful," "My Country, 'Tis of Thee," etc. Since the earliest days of public education, the schools were expected to teach students about the history, culture, and symbols of America and to encourage them to feel part of the nation.

And Ravitch makes an even more telling point connecting the emphasis on patriotism to the multiple ethnicities of American students.

American schools probably went further in their patriotic spirit than the schools of other nations. . . . Other nations are based on ties of blood or religion, but the United States is a social creation, evolving not from common inherited features but from a shared adherence to the democratic ideology embedded in the Declaration of Independence and the Constitution. The public schools were expected to help forge the American people anew in each generation by teaching children about the nature and workings of democratic self-government.

"Liberty and Justice for all" is no narrow concept. The abandonment of American patriotism is a big mistake, not an advance in ethical thinking. In the modern world, the nation is the only universal source of morality and ideals, of laws and community. Lacking a national religion to unify our democratic society, we have no reliable means other than the nation itself for creating a law-abiding, mutually supportive, altruistic moral community from a huge human group. The Founding Fathers claimed a universal human basis for its patriotism: equality, safety, happiness.

That's a universal, not an ethnocentric, ideal, consistent with the equality, safety, and happiness of all citizens of the world. Although blacks did not become full US citizens until 1866, advanced thinkers in the North believed from the time of the founding that the universalistic principles of "all men are created equal" extended to all races, that all could become new men and women on this new continent. Ethnicity is not inborn. We can have two ethnic identities fairly easily. Nature has given us big, blank brains precisely to enable education to form big, powerful societies.

But the great Durkheim, who explained how national societies in modern times have taken over the role of religion, was opposed to extreme nationalism. He favored the American-style universal moral principles governing nations and their interrelations. During the First World War, he wrote a powerful pamphlet called *Germany Over All* (1915), which criticized Germany's hypernationalism. The first line of Germany's national anthem was (and is) "Deutschland über alles" ("Germany above everything"). The German kaiser and chancellor were viewed as supreme rulers whom all Germans must obey. That, Durkheim eloquently wrote, is a *wrong* kind of nationalism. A nation's civil society and its moral principles should rule its head of government, not vice versa; those *principles* are supreme. The government and its leaders are *not* the nation.

Such citizenship-patriotism was the kind Lincoln stressed in the Gettysburg Address when he spoke of "government of the people, by the people, for the people." Those are principles both national *and* universal. For our own well-being, we need to revive patriotism even while repudiating an "America über alles" sort of nationalism. As Theodore Roosevelt said in a 1912 speech in Paris (forgive him his older use of "man" for both sexes):

I believe that a man must be a good patriot before he can be, and as the only possible way of being, a good citizen of the world. Experience teaches us that the average person who protests that his international feeling swamps his national feeling, that he does not care for his country because he cares so much for mankind, in actual practice proves himself the foe of mankind; that the person who says that he does not care to be a citizen of any one country, because he is a citizen of the world, is in very fact usually an exceedingly undesirable citizen of whatever corner of the world he happens at the moment to be in. . . . Now, this does not mean in the least that a person should not wish to do good outside of his native land. On the contrary, just as I think that the person who loves his family is more apt to be a good neighbor than the person who does not, so I think that the most useful member of the family of nations is normally a strongly patriotic nation.

It is this very conception of patriotism that president Theodore Roosevelt (who gave us our national parks) was also articulating when he said early in the twentieth century:

Patriotism means to stand by the country. It does not mean to stand by the president or any other public official, save exactly to the degree in which he himself stands by the country. It is patriotic to support him insofar as he efficiently serves the country. It is unpatriotic not to oppose him to the exact extent that by inefficiency or otherwise he fails in his duty to stand by the country. In either event, it is unpatriotic not to tell the truth, whether about the president or anyone else.

Professor Ravitch (the premier educational historian in the United States) said much the same thing a century later:

> To love one's country does not require one to dismiss the virtues of other countries. Indeed, those who are patriotic about their own country tend to respect those who live elsewhere and also love their respective countries. Our schools need to impart a patriotic sense of obligation and belonging within the country. They need to foster a sense of moral obligation to the well-being of our society as a whole. No community large or small can stay healthy otherwise. Competence and community: both are necessary to keep our large, heterogeneous nation healthy and unified.

As Durkheim understood, patriotism is the state religion of the modern nation. But, in the United States, our blood is the "blood of the whole world," as Melville put it. Patriotism is the universal civil religion that our schools need to support on moral and pragmatic grounds as the glue that holds us together and forbids us to injure one another. Patriotism gives universal sentiments a poetic concreteness that makes it work emotionally. It offers brotherhood and sisterhood. Liberty, Equality, and Kindness—our version of that great triple motto of the French Revolution.

The Common School and Citizen Making

As Yuval Harari's brilliantly learned book *Sapiens* points out, the socializing and ultimately the nationalizing of *Homo sapiens* has proved to be a powerful evolutionary device to defeat its enemies. It is also a peaceable and happy arrangement *if* the education of the young is wise and effective and is, in these days, also international and peaceable. For schooling to achieve that kind of beneficent result, adults are obliged to hand down the tribe's language and customs, so the child benefits from their historically gained wisdom.

Absent a national religion, the school takes on the task of defining social morality and the ethics of tribal membership. Without a common medium of spiritual exchange, along with strong commitments to one another, no modern nation could exist. Allegiance to the tribe and its distant inhabitants can be sustained only by the school-based ability to weld distant people into a cohesive social unit. Print and print languages enable a population to communicate at a distance. When these elements are present, the modern nation becomes a formidable organism at the apex of evolution.

Equality and Kindness

The emotional sentiment of American tribal unity—of regarding all our citizens as full members of the American tribe—will help reverse the sense of alienation and the rising suicide rate in the United States (up some 30 percent in the last decade). It will also enhance progress in social and economic justice. These aims can be accomplished only by a society whose members possess an emotional commitment to their fellow citizens developed in early life, not just an abstract humanitarianism developed in adulthood.

Our American values of liberty and equality apply to all of our inhabitants. Melville's claim that you can't spill a drop of American blood without spilling the blood of the whole world is a poet's way of saying that *our* ethnicity—our principles and our "blood"—are universal in character. Like the ship's crew in *Moby-Dick,* we come from all over the world. On that ship, the *Pequod*, the language spoken is English. Our universal democratic principles must be stated in *some* particular shared language. Our universals *happen* to be stated in "the language of Britain," to use Melville's phrase. The most effective and productive way for an interest group to achieve fairness in America is not to come across as separate in terms of ethnicity, gender, specialness, or entitlement; these are all based on interest-group politics. It's more effective politically to present oneself as an American who wants to be treated fairly by other Americans.

That name, "American," has fully become the name of an *ethnos*. *Ethnos* means "nation" in Greek. The American version is fully as much an ethnicity as any other. As part of our avowed adherence to universal principles, our elementary schools have a fundamental duty to educate *all* children into our *specific* American ethnicity

No matter what a child's *other* ethnicities and origins and ancestries might be, our American schools are inherently obliged to teach everyone the specific culture of our specific public sphere, so that all become fully *Citizen* Americans as well as Afro Americans, Native Americans, lesbian Americans, Democrat Americans, Chinese Americans. Yes, let a thousand ethnicities bloom, but not in the shared national public sphere, where communication and effective action—that is, citizenship—must go into effect.

Our schools need to teach that "American" is a full-fledged unhyphenated ethnic category like any other. Toni Morrison with her usual acuteness saw the racist implications in those hyphens. She said, "In this country American means white. Everybody else has to hyphenate." Our teachers need to say, "To heck with hyphens." Morrison implied briefly and bitingly that the term "American" has been illegitimately racialized, and that accurate thinkers and persons of goodwill should not use the concept of ethnicity in a muddy, euphemistic, evasive, and implicitly racist way. To stay conscious of the difference between culture and race will also have the beneficial effect of elevating "American" into the full-fledged ethnicity that it inherently is. On this new continent every person can write the American ethnicity on his or her receptive and even rewritable blank slate. And the person who teaches us this new writing is chiefly the elementary school teacher.

It's a deep shame that our idealistic elementary teachers are being thrown into confusion by the half-baked educational theories that took the United States by storm in the early twentieth century. Those theories assumed that children have a nature that needs to be honored and followed. On the contrary, our grade school teachers need to know that they are the makers and remakers of that nature; that they stand in the tradition of their great predecessors Noah Webster and Horace Mann; that they are the preservers of American solidarity and unity, and idealism. But alas, surveys show a "precipitous drop" in teachers' job satisfaction since 2009 and an "undercurrent of despair" about their work. This is a profound misfortune for teachers and the nation. There is no more satisfying or important job in any nation than that of the elementary school teacher. In Plato's *Republic*, the "Guardians" were deemed the most important protectors of the nation. In the spiritual sphere of the modern nation, schoolteachers are the guardians of the nation—the citizen makers.

In the current demoralized context, teachers' unions, and teachers themselves, need to raise their voices. They should not have the impossible burden of deciding what children shall be learning in each grade, just because our state leaders are averse to controversy. *Their* irresponsibility leads to a content incoherence that is not the teachers' doing. Teachers should be told exactly what the grade-by-grade shared content needs to be. Then teachers can exercise their professional skills in effective teaching to eager and proud future citizens. Such shared, value-laden knowledge is the only firm foundation for social communication in a nation. Shared knowledge is the only foundation for competence, for equality of opportunity and the renewal of the American Dream. The liberation of teachers to be citizen makers is to offer them the ultimate in honor and vocational meaningfulness within a democracy—to be the guardians in chief of the American future. Only then will the children in our elementary schools cease to be deprived of their birthright as Americans.

Afterword: What Can Be Done Right Now?

Parents of children in public schools (regular or charter) feel hopeless to change those entrenched institutions. In truth, they could not change overnight even if they wanted to. But we must not give up. Not only is your child's future at stake, but so is that of our nation. How much longer can we prosper when our schools now rank twenty-fourth in the world? You as a parent will need the support of receptive teachers and principals. You will need the support of fellow citizens in your location. Our Core Knowledge Foundation is tiny, but as an emergency measure it can supply your school with free downloadable materials if it wants to take the leap. But ultimately, states will need to get specific. Patriotic citizens need to unite to inform our state legislatures, enlighten their minds, and stiffen their spines.

On their own initiative, our elementary schools can start improving overnight, now that we are able to introduce parents, teachers, and principals to instant videos of top principals and teachers who can explain exactly how they achieved their thrilling successes in severely disadvantaged neighborhoods in every part of the country. But effective as these teachers and principals have been in achieving what they set out to do in educating young children, they have been unsuccessful in changing the minds and the behavior of the adults in charge of their school districts.

That is because our districts have been trapped in a web of ideas and slogans that still govern the minds of our education professors and hence the minds of teachers and administrators. Those ideas endure powerfully because they reflect at bottom a powerful religious conviction that "nature knows best." As we've seen from the stories in this book of kids growing up in poverty and *consistently* emerging with top results by eighth grade, nature *isn't* really saying what John Dewey and our schools of education thought it was saying. These kids *prove* that we can turn this around and get all students on a level playing field.

I began this book with very encouraging descriptions of regular public schools in Alexandria, Virginia, and in Riverside, California, followed by an account of Jeffrey Litt's astonishing seven schools in the heart of the South Bronx. These stories show what can be accomplished in raising student competence by teaching a knowledge-coherent curriculum based on the knowledge that tends to be shared among literate Americans.

Let me end with a report that is just in from rural Appalachia—Sullivan County, Tennessee, where 60 percent of the students are economically deprived. *These are results not from a single school but from an entire district.* The gains are by far the largest ever recorded in the district, and they are remarkable, coming as they are after just a few months. They were achieved by introducing a language arts program created by the Core Knowledge Foundation, formed from the Core Knowledge

Sequence of shared topics. The report by the district's elementary supervisor, Robin McClellan, is from the Kingsport, Tennessee, *Times News*. Here's an excerpt:

In this year's spring screening, Sullivan County students showed historic gains in reading.

Decreased Number of Students Identified as At-Risk Readers

The district achieved a significant decrease in the number of students with "at-risk" levels of reading proficiency, from 37.8% of students in the fall screening to 26% in the spring screening. This means that the district has 456 fewer elementary students with an "at-risk" designation for reading. The gains were most pronounced in first and second grade, which saw a 19% and 14% decrease of at-risk students respectively.

All 11 elementary schools in the district saw decreases in the number of at-risk students. Bluff City Elementary School showed particularly strong data, with approximately 30% fewer students considered to be "at-risk" in kindergarten and 20% fewer students considered to be "at-risk" in first grade.

Increased Number of Students Performing at Top Levels

Across all grades, more Sullivan County students scored in the top range of performance. As evidenced by the fall screening, 15.2% of students were in the 75–100th percentile compared to national benchmarks, and in the spring screening, 22.1% of students were scoring in the highest percentile band.

Overall, the picture is one of improved performance across all segments, from high-achieving to lower-achieving student populations. According to Christy Nelson, K–5 instructional coach, "Our students have made exponential growth moving out of the at-risk designation. Additionally, more students are scoring in the highest percentile band, which indicates that strong curriculum in the hands of teachers committed to student growth meets the needs of all learners."

The curriculum, Core Knowledge Language Arts[,] or CKLA, is designed to engage students with rich science and history topics while they grow as readers who are building background knowledge. Students read interesting books about those subjects, participate in detailed discussions, complete projects, and/or write about the topics.

This district recognized a problem and made a significant commitment to fix it—by investing in a new curriculum *and* the teacher training needed to implement it.

If this kind of progress can be made in Appalachia by an entire district, it can be made anywhere. By eighth grade, with a coherent knowledge-based curriculum in all subjects, these children, just like Litt's students in the South Bronx, could be winning debate contests in Memphis or Richmond

No first-rate education system in the world evades the logic of an agreed-on national sequence of core topics in elementary school. It is self-defeating to evade this logic, which represents a kind of unilateral intellectual disarmament in a competitive world. Now that we have the knowledge, future generations will find it unforgivable that we did nothing, particularly as we are a nation whose greatness owes itself to our idealism and our pragmatism.

We have example after example of schools bucking the odds because they've turned to a shared-knowledge curriculum, but the image I keep returning to in my mind is the one I'll leave you with: the disadvantaged students who beat out the most advantaged districts in New York and New Jersey at the American Debate League Middle School City Championships. I've listened to these students talk about what this has done for their confidence and their excitement about learning, and I'm happy to have been a part of their educational journey. I hope that their message can also deeply impress school administrators, teachers, parents, and voters in every school district in the nation, because it's time for an educational revolution!

Acknowledgments

If this book succeeds in persuading devoted teachers and administrators in our elementary schools, and the parents of these children, it will be because I have had a lot of help in writing it. My intellectual debts are many and are acknowledged along the way. But I have deep personal debts, too, in writing this book.

Thanks first to Joel Klein, the former chancellor of the New York City Department of Education, the largest public school system in the United States. Joel not only persuaded me to keep working at improving the presentation, but also gave me the courage to be more forthright and less polite to the disabling ideas that have lamed our nation's schools.

Thanks to John Hirsch, my literary son, who supplied, among other excellent tips, the phrase "the Power of Shared Knowledge." That's it in a nutshell.

Thanks to Natasha Tobin, my dear wife, who has read every word, and, as a nonacademic, told me exactly where I was not being clear or persuasive.

Thanks to John Ballen, chairman of the board of the Core Knowledge Foundation, who loyally read, advised, and encouraged this book in its many phases.

Thanks to Marly Rusoff, my book agent, who stuck by this project during its long gestation.

Thanks to Jenna Glatzer, who offered excellent and detailed editorial shaping of the book.

And thanks to the best editor of my long experience, Gail Winston, whose advice has been decisive in making this a more readable and cogent book.

Thanks to the team members at the Core Knowledge Foundation, led by Linda Bevilacqua, who have kept me informed throughout with bulletins from the schools.

Thanks to Michele Hudak and Cathy Kinter, two wonderful Core Knowledge teachers who had long taught in both kinds of schools, and who essentially composed chapter 2.

And thanks to other heroes in the schools, some acknowledged in the book, but many hundreds more unnamed, who, to the benefit of their young students, have bravely put into exemplary practice what we as a country need to do if we are to fulfill our promise as a nation for all. Our schools are the chief agents of that vision of unity. The idea of a shared American identity needs to make a comeback, liberated from any taint of narrow ethnicity or race. Being American is our common and most essential "identity."

Notes

CHAPTER 1 When Our Schools Abandoned Commonality, We Became a Nation at Risk

4   Ethnicity and nationality: The recent remarkable findings about "cortical plasticity" are discussed in part II of the present work.

5   71 percent of Americans: Henry L. Roediger III and K. Andrew DeSoto, "Recognizing the Presidents: Was Alexander Hamilton President?," *Psychological Science* 27, no. 5 (May 2016): 644–50, https://doi.org/10.1177/0956797616631113.

5   "The bonds of national cohesion": Arthur M. Schlesinger Jr., *The Disuniting of America* (New York: Norton, 1992), 119–39.

6   Émile Durkheim was right: My translation of Durkheim's remarkable, recently discovered lecture to schoolteachers (ca. 1912) is posted on the website for this book: http://educatecitizens.net/, along with my introduction. A similar argument about the nation-state being the largest effective political society was made independently by Richard Rorty in his book *Achieving Our Country: Leftist Thought in Twentieth-Century America* (Cambridge: Harvard University Press, 1998), 98ff. Current history continues to support their analysis, as well as that of Karl W. Deutsch in *Nationalism and Social Communication: An Inquiry into the Foundations of Nationality* (Cambridge: Technology Press of the Massachusetts Institute of Technology; New York: Wiley, 1953): that the modern nation-state is the largest practical *political* society.

6   Teddy Roosevelt was deeply right: His remarks are quoted and discussed in chapter 9, on patriotism.

9   "The Education of youth": Noah Webster, "On the Education of Youth in America," in *A Collection of Essays and Fugitive Writings on Moral, Historical, Political, and Literary Subjects* (Boston, 1790).

10   A fundamental mistake of the Americans: "Remarks on the Manners, Government, and Debt of the United States," in *A Collection of Essays and Fugitive Writings*.

12   Be Kind: Noah Webster, *An American Speller*, 1807 edition, 51.

13   "the largest sale": Quoted in *The Chariton* [Iowa] *Patriot*, May, 26, 1880, C5.

13   The Yorkshireman cannot: Quoted in Harlow G. Unger, *Noah Webster: The Life and Times of an American Patriot*, (New York: Wiley, 1998), 17.

17   "We have chosen": Introduction to the graded series edited by Franklin Baker, Ashley H. Thorndike, et al., *Everyday Classics* (New York: Macmillan, 1936, plus many ed.)

20   Our birth is but: William Wordsworth, "Ode: Intimations of Immortality Upon Recollections of Early Childhood," *Poems in Two Volumes*. Reprinted from the original 1807 edition, with a note on the Wordsworth sonnet by Thomas Hutchinson (London, England: D. Nutt, 1897).

21   The Child is: Wordsworth, "My Heart Leaps Up," *Poems in Two Volumes*.

21   *A Nation at Risk: The Imperative for Educational Reform:* See a digitized version of the report at: https://babel.hathitrust.org/cgi/pt?id=mdp.3901 5004170224&view=1up&seq=17: National Commission on Excellence in Education, *A Nation at Risk: The Imperative for Educational Reform* (Washington, DC: US Government Printing Office, 1983), 5.

22   Here's a picture: See, for instance, Richard C. Atkinson and Saul Geiser, "Reflections on a Century of College Admissions Tests," *Educational Researcher* 38, no. 9 (December 2009): 665–76, https://doi.org/10.3102/0013189X09351981.

26   In retrospect: This insight of psycholinguistics is the finding that has presided over my theoretical work since the 1960s. It began in my 1967 book *Validity in Interpretation* (Yale University Press, 1967). Background knowledge enables very complex meanings to be communicated in short space. The fundamental insight throws into a cocked hat the scientifically questionable standard of "complexity" in the Common Core State Standards for language arts. That is a naïve "standard" put in place to avoid the hard and brave work of specifying tribal content that will enable all children to understand the language of print, internet, and mass media. Psychological complexity derives far more from silent ignorance than from the form of spoken or written words.

28   "We have really": Oscar Wilde, *The Canterville Ghost,* 1887 (Boston: J. W. Luce and Co. 1906).

28   The great scholar: Deutsch, *Nationalism and Social Communication*. A second edition of the book (Cambridge, MA: MIT Press, 1966) adds a short introduction but few new ideas—except this one: With all the efforts of empire and of international unions (Deutsch was an important participant in the forming of the United Nations), the nation-state seems destined to remain the chief vehicle for "getting things done," a view shared by Émile Durkheim half a century earlier and Richard Rorty half a century later. (In *Achieving Our Country* Rorty argued that patriotism is essential in any nation, because the nation is the optimal unit for getting things done [100–103].)

29　Now you understand: In particular, you now understand the power of unstated, unmentioned shared knowledge. Its nonexplicit presence is the reason that its essential power in securing the unity and competence of a nation has too often gone unnoticed. Economic globalism (ruled by efficiency of transport and the transmission of information) is no substitute for social cooperation and the basic morality that counteracts innate selfishness and sadism—two impulses that weaken the effectiveness of social groups. Deutsch's great book seems rarely mentioned these days.

CHAPTER 2 **The Child-Centered Classroom**

33　Maintain consistency in style: The inutility of vague standards like these is an intellectual and technical scandal. It's equivalent to saying, "Teach children to read and write well. We'll generously leave it up to you teachers how to do it."

35　Yes, yes. I told: Throughout these chapters I use the generic terms "child centered" and "knowledge centered." The actual terms used by Ms. Hudak and Ms. Kinter were "child-centered schools" and "core-knowledge schools," since they are both core-knowledge teachers. But this book is not an advertisement for any particular manifestation of a shared-knowledge curriculum, but rather an argument for the importance of a shared-knowledge curriculum. So I have inserted the phrase "knowledge-centered schools" when they used the phrase "core knowledge schools." Core knowledge is just an example of the *kind* of curriculum that needs to be instituted in the United States.

CHAPTER 3 **"Nobody Leaves": The Dazzling Success of Shared-Knowledge Schools**

62　half a standard deviation: That is a big, decisive statistical difference between large, randomly assigned groups of schoolchildren. Here is how Matt di Carlo at the Albert Shanker Institute describes the relative significance of standard-deviation percentages in educational studies: "In charter school studies, it's unusual to find effects larger than 0.20 to 0.30 of a standard deviation, and most are between zero and 0.10." In other words, 0.5 of a standard deviation is a very significant improvement. It betokens a life-changing effect-size for these children. See Matt di Carlo, "What Is a Standard Deviation?" at www.shankerinstitute.org.

62　These are decisive results: The results were reported by Professor Grissmer in a recent public lecture at a school conference in Denver. I eagerly await publication!

66　honored by New York State: More recently, *six* of the seven core knowledge schools in the South Bronx have been identified as "Recognition

Schools"—a new category of recognition for schools that have "met or exceeded either the school or state measures of interim progress for English language arts and mathematics, rate of Chronic Absenteeism, and College, Career, and Civic Readiness." See: http://www.nysed .gov/news/2019/state-education-department-identifies-562-recognition -schools.

67 its chief moral and social precept: Ms. Durant is quoted on the relationship between "kindness" and "patriotism" in an epigraph to chapter 9 (p. 177).

70 We believe that: https://www.successacademies.org/app/uploads/2018 /05/es-curriculum-guide.pdf.

74 download it for free: https://www.coreknowledge.org/curriculum /download-curriculum/.

76 effective speech community is formed: A "speech community" can be defined as a group that lends verbal utterances to very similar cognitive and emotional meanings. That is possible only when the members of the community share the same relevant background knowledge and values.

CHAPTER 4 The Problem Starts at Our Teacher-Training Institutes

78 His hugely influential 1918 paper "The Project Method": This paper is still in print as a booklet.

79 "Progressive education in the 1940s": https://www.youtube.com/watch ?v=opXKmwg8VQM. Posted by Daniel Mitchell.

79 In an opinion piece: Emily Hanford, "Why Are We Still Teaching Reading the Wrong Way?," *New York Times*, October 26, 2018, https://www .nytimes.com/2018/10/26/opinion/sunday/phonics-teaching-reading -wrong-way.html.

83 "Selfishness beats altruism": David Sloan Wilson and E. O. Wilson, "Rethinking the Theoretical Foundations of Sociobiology," *Quarterly Review of Biology* 82, no. 4 (December 2007): 327–48, https://doi.org /10.1086/522809.

84 "My Pedagogic Creed": First published in *The School Journal*, LIV, no. 3 (January 16, 1897), pp. 77–80.

85 *How We Think* (1910): http://www.gutenberg.org/files/37423/37423-h /37423-h.htm. "Preface" p. 1.

88 Constructivism in mainline psychology: For a good, brief account on what is valid scientifically in constructivism, see Reg Dennick, "Constructivism: Reflections on Twenty-Five Years Teaching the Constructivist Approach, in Medical Education," *International Journal of Medical Education* 2 (June 25, 2016): 200–205, https://doi.org/10.5116 /ijme.5763.de11. Dennick usefully quotes the psychologist David P. Ausubel from his book *Educational Psychology: A Cognitive View* (New York:

Holt, Rinehart and Winston, 1968): "The most important factor influencing learning is what the learner already knows."

92   "In 1982 I began": Diane Ravitch, "Tot Sociology: Or What Happened to History in the Grade Schools," *American Scholar* 56, no. 3 (Summer 1987): 345–54.

93   "Expanding environments is": Kathleen Porter-Magee, James Leming, and Lucien Ellington, *Where Did Social Studies Go Wrong?* (Washington, DC: Thomas B. Fordham Institute, 2003), 112, https://fordham institute.org/national/research/where-did-social-studies-go-wrong.

96   "The education our teachers": Arthur Levine, *Educating School Teachers*, The Education School Project, 2006, 19, http://edschools.org/pdf /Educating_Teachers_Report.pdf.

96   a decisive article: Paul A. Kirschner, John Sweller, and Richard E. Clark, "Why Minimal Guidance During Instruction Does Not Work: An Analysis of the Failure of Constructivist, Discovery, Problem-Based, Experiential, and Inquiry-Based Teaching," *Educational Psychologist* 41, no. 2 (2006): 76–86, https://doi.org/10.1207/s15326985ep 4102_1.

100   "After a half century": Richard E. Clark, Paul A. Kirschner, and John Sweller, "Putting Students on the Path to Learning: The Case for Fully Guided Instruction," *American Educator*, Spring 2012, 6–11, https://www .aft.org/sites/default/files/periodicals/Clark.pdf.

CHAPTER 5 **Culture, Not Nature, Knows Best—Says Nature**

105   bullying and misguided phrase: For a rough gauge of the mental harm that is *not* caused by early knowledge-intensive schooling, we could compare the mental illness rates of Singapore and the United States. The rate of mental illness in Singapore is 37 percent lower than in the USA. See Ronald C. Kessler et al., "The Global Burden of Mental Disorders: An Update from the WHO World Mental Health (WMH) Surveys," *Epidemiology and Psychiatric Sciences* 18, no. 1 (March 2009): 23–33, https://doi.org/10.1017/S1121189X00001421.

105   Evolution has worked: David Sloan Wilson and E. O. Wilson, "Re-thinking the Theoretical Foundations of Sociobiology," *Quarterly Review of Biology* 82, no. 4 (December 2007): 327–48, https://doi.org/10.1086 /522809.

106   largely a blank slate: The word "largely" should be noted by the reader. Some centers of the vast neocortex must be structured in advance—especially the language centers, as Steven Pinker and others have argued.

108   published an article: Nir Kalisman, Gilad Silberberg, and Henry Markram, "The Neocortical Microcircuit as a *Tabula Rasa*," *Proceedings*

of the National Academy of Science 102, no. 3 (January 2005): 880–85, https://doi.org/10.1073/pnas.0407088102.

109 We evolved not only: Eszter Boldog et al., "Transcriptomic and Morphophysiological Evidence for a Specialized Huma Cortical GABAergic Cell Type," *Nature Neuroscience* 21 (September 2018): 1185–95, https://doi.org/10.1038/s41593-018-0205-2.

110 recent studies of cortical plasticity: Sally A. Marik and Charles D. Gilbert, "Cortical Plasticity," in *The Oxford Handbook of Developmental Neural Plasticity*, ed. M. Chao (online: Oxford University Press, April 2018), https://10.1093/oxfordhb/9780190635374.013.8.

110 Our Constitution was formed: *Federalist*, no. 55 (James Madison).

112 The essentializing of ethnicity: See Leigh S. Wilton, Evan P. Apfelbaum, and Jessica J. Good, "Valuing Differences and Reinforcing Them: Multiculturalism Increases Race Essentialism," *Social Psychological and Personality Science* 10, no. 5 (July 2019): 681–89, https://doi.org/10.1177/1948550618780728.

114 the Academy released a book: National Research Council, *How People Learn: Brain, Mind, Experience, and School*, expanded edition (Washington, DC: National Academies Press, 2000), https://doi.org/10.17226/9853.

114 released a second volume: National Research Council, *How People Learn II: Learners, Contexts, and Cultures* (Washington, DC: National Academies Press, 2018), https://doi.org/10.17226/24783.

116 New York City: https://www.schools.nyc.gov/about-us/vision-and-mission/framework-for-great-schools.

116 Chicago: https://cps.edu/STEM/Pages/stem.aspx.

116 "A crucial fact": Anders Ericsson and Robert Poole, *Peak: Secrets from the New Science of Expertise* (Boston: Eamon Dolan, 2016).

118 "One of the major": Teun A. van Dijk and Walter Kintsch, *Strategies of Discourse Comprehension* (New York: Academic Press, 1983).

119 "Each subject silently": Donna Recht and Lauren Leslie, "Effect of Prior Knowledge on Good and Poor Readers' Memory of Text," *Journal of Educational Psychology* 80, no. 1 (March 1988): 16–20, https://doi.org/10.1037/0022-0663.80.1.16.

120 Resulting book by De Groot: Adriaan de Groot, *Thought and Choice in Chess* (The Hague: Mouton, 1965).

122 "Our understanding of": Paul A. Kirschner, John Sweller, and Richard E. Clark, "Why Minimal Guidance During Instruction Does Not Work: An Analysis of the Failure of Constructivist, Discovery, Problem-Based, Experiential, and Inquiry-Based Teaching," *Educational Psychologist* 41, no. 2 (2006): 76, https://doi.org/10.1207/s15326985ep4102_1.

123 "We are skillful": Kirschner, Sweller, and Clark, "Why Minimal Guidance Does Not Work," 76–77.

CHAPTER 6 **The Lessons of Educational Failure and Success around the World**

134   and with similar justification: See especially Laurent Lafforgue and Liliane Lurçat, ed., *Le debacle de l'école,: une tragedie incomprise* (Paris: Guibert, 2007).

CHAPTER 7 **Commonality in a Multiethnic Nation**

147   most important early essays: This was "Thoughts upon the Mode of Education Proper in a Republic, from 1786." In it, Rush stressed the special need for the schools to inculcate patriotism in a republic where the people rule. It was a plea for training nobility of character and loyalty to the society. He foreshadowed the insight of Durkheim, that with modernity and democracy we are forced to grasp that "society" has always been the god behind all religions. Thus Rush: "A Christian, I say again, cannot fail of being a republican, for every precept of the Gospel inculcates those degrees of humility, self-denial, and brotherly kindness which are directly opposed to the pride of monarchy and the pageantry of a court. A Christian cannot fail of being useful to the republic, for his religion teacheth him that no man 'liveth to himself.'" All the thoughtful theorists of the founding invoked history to argue that the republic could endure only if citizens were educated to secular loyalty and virtue on the analogy of religious commandments without narrow religious tribalism.

148   "to spread systematic": https://en.wikisource.org/wiki/Last_Will_and_Testament_of_George_Washington.

148   "Our plan prescribes": Thomas Jefferson, *Notes on the State of Virginia* (1785).

149   "the printing of large": *Documents of the Assembly of the State of New York* (Albany, New York, 1847), 22.

150   "It cannot be doubted": Alexis de Tocqueville, *Democracy in America*, trans. Henry Reese (1847), 355.

151   "On the careful cultivation": *Annual Report of the Superintendent of Common Schools of the State of New York* (Albany, New York, 1845), 19.

152   March of Time movie-short: "New Schools for Old," November 6, 1936. See, for example, "Progressive Education in the 1940s," YouTube video, 7:16, posted by "danieljbmitchell," July 31, 2007, https://www.youtube.com/watch?v=opXKmwg8VQM.

156   the nation-state is the: Karl Deutsch, *Nationalism and Social Communication*, 2nd ed. (Cambridge: MIT Press, 1966), 4.

156   Durkheim stated in a 1910: Émile Durkheim, "L'enseignement de la morale à l'école primaire," *Revue française de sociologie*, XXXIII/4, (1992), 609–623, http://www.persee.fr/doc/rfsoc_035-2969_1992_num_33_4_5627.

157   "For the teaching of morality": My translation of this newly discovered talk is to be found at www.how-to-educate-a-citizen.com.

CHAPTER 8 How to Improve the "Common Core"

164   "I came across": John Riddle, "How to Make Money Writing for School Library Publishers!," WritersWeekly.com, July 19, 2018, https://www.writersweekly.com/this-weeks-article/school-library-publishers.

170   Core Knowledge English Language Arts program: Both the sequence and the language arts program can be downloaded for free from the Core Knowledge Foundation at www.coreknowledge.org.

CHAPTER 9 Patriotism: Shared Knowledge and Kindness

179   "Until the last generation": Diane Ravitch, "Should We Teach Patriotism?," *Phi Delta Kappan* 86, no. 8 (April 2006): 578–81, https://doi.org/10.1177/003172170608700806.

181   "I believe that a man": "Citizenship in a Republic," Speech at the Sorbonne, Paris, April 23, 1910, *The Works of Theodore Roosevelt*, Vol XIII, 506–29.

182   Theodore Roosevelt: https://www.snopes.com/tachyon/2020/01/lincoln-and-free-speech.png.

183   Professor Ravitch . . . said: "Should We Teach Patriotism?" *Phi Delta Kappan* 87, no. 8 (2006), https://doi.org/10.1177/003172170608700806.

184   up some 30 percent: Reported by the Centers for Disease Control, https://www.cdc.gov/vitalsigns/suicide/.

185   It's more effective politically: See Richard Rorty, *Achieving Our Country: Leftist Thought in Twentieth-Century America* (Cambridge, MA: Harvard University Press, 1998): "The pre-Sixties reformist left, insofar as it concerned itself with oppressed minorities did so by proclaiming that all of us—black, white, and brown—are Americans, and that we should respect one another as such. This strategy gave rise to the 'platoon' movies which showed Americans of various ethnic backgrounds fighting and dying side by side. By contrast, the contemporary cultural left urges that America should not be a melting pot, because we need to respect one another in our differences. This Left wants to preserve otherness rather than ignore it. . . . Insofar as this prevents someone from also taking pride in being an American citizen . . . from being able to join with straights or whites in reformist initiatives, it is a political disaster" (100). Rorty speaks not just for the "Old Left" but also for all of the Enlightenment, from Benjamin Rush to the present. The romanticizing of ethnicity *is* indeed a political disaster. It's also a moral failure, and a scientific mistake.

186   a "precipitous drop": Doris A. Santoro, "Is it Burnout? Or Demoralization?," *Educational Leadership* 75, no. 9 (June 2018): 10–15, https://www.ascd.org/publications/educational-leadership/summer18/vol75/num09/Is-It-Burnout%C2%A2-Or-Demoralization%C2%A2.aspx.

Index

About the Author

E. D. Hirsch, Jr. is the founder and chairman of the Core Knowledge Foundation and professor emeritus of education and humanities at the University of Virginia. He is the author of several acclaimed books on education, including the *New York Times* bestseller *Cultural Literacy*, *The Schools We Need*, *The Knowledge Deficit*, *The Making of Americans*, and *Why Knowledge Matters*. A highly regarded literary critic and professor of English earlier in his career, he has persisted as a voice of reason in making the case for equality of educational opportunity.